Speaking Personally

Speaking Personally

Quizzes and questionnaires for fluency practice

Gillian Porter Ladousse

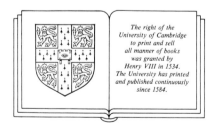

Cambridge University Press
Cambridge
London   New York   New Rochelle
Melbourne   Sydney

Published by the Press Syndicate of the University of Cambridge
The Pitt Building, Trumpington Street, Cambridge CB2 1RP
32 East 57th Street, New York, NY 10022, USA
10 Stamford Road, Oakleigh, Melbourne 3166, Australia

© Cambridge University Press 1983

First published 1983
Reprinted 1984

Printed in Great Britain
at the University Press, Cambridge

ISBN 0 521 28869 X

Copyright
The law allows a reader to make a single copy of part of a book
for purposes of private study. It does not allow the copying of
entire books or the making of multiple copies of extracts. Written
permission for any such copying must always be obtained from the
publisher in advance.

MX

Contents

Introduction   1

1 You and your image   2

2 The future lies in your hands   8

3 How honest are you?   13

4 Food and fitness   20

5 Life's tensions   28

6 A taste of taste   34

7 Brain fever   40

8 Beyond reason   48

9 Your pen personality   57

10 Our families, our friends   68

11 Left, right and centre   80

12 Laughing matters   86

Answers and scoring instructions   99

Guidelines for teachers and students working alone   105
To the student   105
To the teacher   106
   General guidelines   106
   Types of exercise   107
   Notes on individual units   110
   Useful language sections   111
Theme, function and structure chart   113

Acknowledgements

The author and publishers are grateful to the authors, publishers and others who have given permission for the use of copyright material identified in the text. It has not been possible to identify the sources of all the material used and in such cases the publishers would welcome information from copyright owners.

Tessa Sayle for the cartoon on p. 2 from *The Square Egg*, Penguin, © 1968 by Ronald Searle; *Woman's Realm* for the extract on p. 9 by David Brandon-Jones; W. Foulsham & Co Ltd for the extract on pp. 11–12; *Ladies' Home Journal* for the extract on p. 13, © 1979 by LHJ Publishing, Inc.; Chilton Book Company for the extracts on pp. 17 and 34–6 from *Test Yourself* © 1962 by William Bernard and Jules Leopold; Le Nouvel Observateur for the cartoon on p. 21 by Claire Bretecher; Michael Joseph Ltd for the tables on pp. 22 and 32 from *The Sunday Times Book of Body Maintenance* edited by Oliver Gillie and Derrick Mercer; Le Point for the table on p. 26; Perigee Books for the extract on p. 40 from *More Creative Growth Games* © 1980 by Eugene Raudsepp; Usborne Publishing Ltd for the form on p. 52 from *The World of the Unknown* by Ted Wilding-White; Macdonald & Co (Publishers) Ltd for the extract on pp. 53–5 from *Understanding Yourself* by C. Evans, © 1977 Phoebus Publishing Company/BPC Publishing Ltd; Kate Loewenthal for the extracts on p. 61 which first appeared in *New Society*; Jon Swallow for the letter on p. 62; the BBC for the advertisement on p. 66; MAD for the tables on pp. 68–71, © 1966 by E.C. Publications, Inc.; Pan Books Ltd for the extract on pp. 74–6 from *The Personality Test* by Peter Lauster; Ross Speirs for the cartoon on p. 79; *The Observer* for the letter on p. 82; Donald Godden and J.L. Hendeles for the letters on p. 83 which appeared in *The Guardian*; A.D. Peters & Co Ltd for the cartoon on p. 84 by Posy Simmonds; *The New Yorker* for the cartoons on pp. 86, 90 and 92; *Punch* for the cartoons on pp. 88–93 and the extract on pp. 97–8; Methuen London for the cartoons on pp. 91 and 93 from *The Effluent Society* by Norman Thelwell; *Mayfair* for the cartoon on p. 94.

The photographs on page 18 were taken by Nigel Luckhurst; the drawings on page 31 are by Chris Evans. Book designed by Peter Ducker MSTD

Introduction

Speaking Personally aims to help learners improve their competence in social communication skills. This is achieved in various ways, as the material is intentionally flexible in design. It can be used by adult learners at any point beyond that rather ill-defined moment of language learning, the intermediate stage.

Underlying the material is the conviction that people will learn more readily and efficiently if they are actively and personally involved in their language lessons. Thus, throughout the units, the learners are encouraged to react individually to questions concerning many aspects of their daily lives and to discuss and evaluate the part they play in society.

Readers will notice some inconsistencies in spelling according to whether the source of the activity is British or American.

The material is designed to be used either in the classroom or by the student working alone. The symbol ☆ indicates activities which students can work through on their own but they may find further ideas for self-study in much of the group work. At the end of the book the teacher will find suggestions on how to use the units in class.

The book may be used as a short revision course in oral skills or as a complement to a course book. A chart on page 113 indicates how the units and activities can be linked up with general course work.

While developing the material I have shared in a great deal of fun with students, colleagues and friends. I thank them all for their participation and hope that you may share some of the fun.

G.P.L.

1 You and your image

1.1 Do you see yourself as others see you? ☆

Work through this quiz with a partner.

Do other people see you as you see yourself?

It is no good looking into a mirror if you wish to see the person who is *really* you. The only real test is to see yourself in the same way as other people see you. The following quiz has been psychologically developed to help you to do exactly that...

1. When do you feel your best:
   a) Soon after waking up?
   b) During the afternoon and early evening?
   c) Before you go to bed?

2. Do you usually walk:
   a) Quite fast, with long, swinging steps?
   b) Quite fast, but with short, quick steps?
   c) Not very fast, with your head up, looking at the world?
   d) Not very fast, with your head down?
   e) Very slowly?

3. When you are talking to people, do you:
   a) Stand with your arms folded?
   b) Stand with your hands together in front of you?
   c) Stand with one or both hands on your hips?
   d) Touch the person you are talking to?
   e) Touch your ear or chin or smooth your hair?
   f) Have something like a pencil or a cigarette in your hands?

4. When you are relaxing, do you sit with
   a) Your knees bent and your legs together?
   b) Your legs crossed or wrapped round each other?
   c) Your legs stretched straight out in front of you?
   d) With one leg curled up underneath you?

5. When you find something very funny, how do you react? Do you:
   a) Give a loud, appreciative laugh?
   b) Laugh, but not very loudly?
   c) Laugh softly, under your breath?
   d) Give a very big smile?
   e) Smile slowly?

6. When you go to a party, do you:
   a) Make so much noise as you enter that everybody notices you?
   b) Walk in quietly, looking for someone you know?
   c) Hope that nobody will see you walking in, so you can remain unnoticed?

7 When you are interrupted while you are working hard, concentrating on something, do you:
   a) Feel pleased to be interrupted?
   b) Feel very irritated?
   c) Or do you feel neither of these reactions very strongly?

8 Which of the following colours do you like most:
   a) Red or orange?
   b) White?
   c) Black?
   d) Dark blue or purple?
   e) Yellow or light blue?
   f) Brown, grey or violet?
   g) Green?

9 Just before you go to sleep, when you are lying in bed, do you lie:
   a) Flat out on your back?
   b) Stretched out on your front?
   c) On your side?
   d) With your head under one arm?
   e) With your head under the bedclothes?

10 Do you often dream that you are:
   a) Falling?
   b) Involved in a fight?
   c) Looking for someone or something?
   d) Taking your clothes off or with nothing on at all?
   e) Flying or floating?
   f) Do you dream rarely?
   g) Or do you usually have nice, pleasant dreams?

Now check your score on page 99.

What it means

Over 60: Others see you as someone they should 'handle with care' — vain, self-centered and extremely dominant. They may admire you and wish they could be more like you, are certainly in awe of you, but they don't always trust you and hesitate to become too deeply involved with you.

From 51 to 60: Your friends see you as an exciting, highly volatile, rather impulsive personality; a natural leader, quick to make decisions (though not always the right ones). They see you as bold and venturesome, someone who will try anything — well, almost anything — once; someone who takes a chance and enjoys an adventure. They enjoy being in your company because of the excitement you radiate.

From 41 to 50: Others see you as fresh, lively, charming, amusing and always interesting; someone who is constantly the center of attention, but sufficiently well-balanced not to let it go to your head. They see you also as kind, considerate and understanding, someone who will cheer them up or help them out as the situation requires.

From 31 to 40: Other people see you as sensible, cautious, careful and practical. They see you as clever, gifted or talented, but modest. Not a person who makes friends too quickly or too easily, but someone who is extremely loyal to the friends you do make and who expects the same loyalty in return. Those who really get to know you realise that it takes a lot to shake your trust in your friends, but, equally, that it takes you a long time to get over it if that trust is shaken.

From 21 to 30: Your friends see you as meticulous and painstaking, perhaps a bit too fussy at times, ultra-cautious and ultra-careful, a slow, steady plodder. It would surprise them tremendously if you were ever to behave impulsively or do something on the spur of the moment. They expect you to examine everything very carefully from every conceivable angle and then, usually, decide against it. They see this sort of reaction on your part as being partly due to your careful nature and partly to indolence.

Under 21: You are seen to be shy, nervous and indecisive, someone who needs looking after, who always leaves it to someone else to make the decisions and prefers never to get too involved with anyone or anything. They see you as something of a worrier, seeing problems which don't exist and crossing bridges long before you come to them. Some people tend to regard you as dull and boring and it takes someone who knows you well to know that you are not. The trouble is that you permit very few people to get that close to you.

1.2 Public images and private lives

The image you project is not necessarily permanent. Many people want or have to change their image according to the situations in which they find themselves.

a) With a partner, work out a list of ways in which you might like to change your own image.
b) Role-play: the successful politician
   Before you begin the role-play, discuss what kind of character the politician is, what the political climate is, etc.

POLITICIAN

You are a candidate for an important election and have been told that your chances of success are compromised by your bad public image. You decide to consult a public relations agency to see how this can be changed.

PUBLIC RELATIONS CONSULTANT

You are interviewing a client who is a politician and who needs to change his or her public image before an important election.

Useful language

poise   ambition
self-assurance   lack of self-confidence
self-control   the way you dress

Talking about habits:
   You dress smartly, casually, seductively, badly.
   You stand in a relaxed manner, stiffly.
   You speak clearly, loudly, softly.
   You look sure of yourself, unsure of yourself, ill at ease.
   You walk briskly, slowly.
   You gesticulate a lot. You don't gesticulate enough.

Giving advice: (Here the advice becomes more and more direct.)
   Why don't you try wearing quieter colours?
   You could have your hair restyled.
   You should have your beard trimmed more neatly.
   Try to be less obsequious.

1.3 Mutual impressions

Work in pairs. Choose as a partner someone you know fairly well or someone whose judgement you trust. First, work through the quiz by yourself. Answer the questions twice, once about yourself and once about your partner. When both you and your partner have finished, compare your results.

1. How would the people you work with describe your role in the group?
   - a leader
   - everyone's friend
   - a mother/father figure
   - a good listener
   - a gossip
   - other

2. How would you describe your attitude to your work?
   - enthusiastic
   - compulsive; you can't stop
   - conscientious, but no more
   - a square peg in a round hole
   - frustrated; capable of doing other and better things

3. What is the atmosphere you create in a group?
   - warm
   - chilly
   - stormy
   - foggy
   - strictly from another planet

4. What sort of a boss would you make?
   - so-so
   - domineering
   - perfect
   - definitely not management material

5. Do you:
   - act your age
   - seem much older
   - seem much younger?

6. How do you treat your superiors?
   - with respect
   - with kid gloves
   - as equals
   - with resentment

7 How do you handle your inferiors?

- you are condescending
- you exploit them
- you help them to get on
- you fear the competition they may offer

8 How does work affect your personal life?

- they are two separate worlds
- they complement each other
- work interferes with your personal life

9 How does your personal life affect work?

- you maintain two watertight compartments in your life
- home overflows into your professional life
- home gives you a firm basis from which to cope with the stress of work

10 How do you use opportunities?

- you jump at them
- you use them reasonably
- you are frightened by change
- you never notice them

11 How do you view confrontations?

- you are prepared to fight
- you give way immediately
- you welcome a chance for discussion
- you feel very uncomfortable

12 What first impression do you give?

- you are smart and know what you are doing
- you have a sense of humour
- you are fairly insignificant
- you are out to impress people
- interesting; people would like to know you better

How to score

You get 5 points for every answer about yourself that your partner agrees with. A score of 45 is remarkable. The answers on which you disagree will tell you a surprising amount about how you see yourself and how others see you. Any score below 35 calls for a reappraisal of your image. If you and your partner agree entirely, you either know each other extremely well or are completely predictable. In both cases you should perhaps be thinking of moving on to new challenges.

1.4 Popularity images

Work in pairs. What is it that makes some people the life and soul of the party and others just plain bores? Think of someone you know and consider to be popular and try to work out just what the characteristics are that make him or her so charismatic. Are they the same qualities as those that make certain public figures popular?

1.5 Personal equation cards

Write a description of yourself in such a way that it could be no other person you know. Describe ideas and personality rather than physical appearance. (This can be a good way of finding out if the group you are working in notices what you consider to be the most essential and unique aspects of your personality.) All the cards in the group are then collected in a hat or a box. After they have been mixed up they are read out by one member of the group. The group has to identify who wrote each card. If the group thinks the card might belong to more than one person, or if anyone in the group says 'That's just like me', the author of the card must revise his or her description.

1.6 Discussion

Is the image one projects only important in public life, or is it important in our relationships with our friends and families as well?
Do we pay too much importance to people's images?
Is it morally right that a politician should get more votes simply by appearing less tough or aggressive through training his or her voice and changing hairstyles?
Can one succeed – socially or in a job – if one has not got the 'right' image?
Is there anyone you have got to know and like despite a public image that you found unpleasant?

2 The future lies in your hands

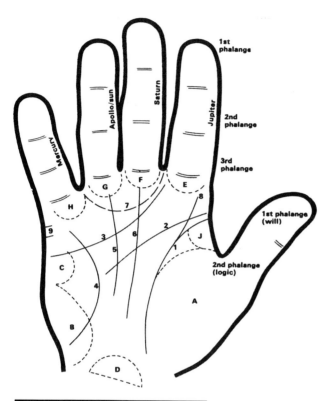

2.1 Reading your palm ☆

It is not very easy to read the lines on your hand itself. The best alternative is to make a photocopy. If you do not have access to a photocopier you can improvise a palm print in the following way.

1 Use a lipstick and a piece of cotton wool. Coat your hand with a layer of lipstick.
2 Take a sheet of good quality paper. With your hand completely relaxed, use the other hand to press it down on the paper.
3 Take a ball-point pen and, holding it upright, outline your hand starting at the wrist. If you have long finger nails, stop outlining when you get to the ends of your fingers, and fill in the true shape of your fingertips after lifting your hand from the paper.
4 Cover your thumb with lipstick again, press it onto the paper and outline with the pen.

Analyse the lines in your hand using the following information.
Compare notes with other people.

1   **Life line:** a long, clear life line, with no breaks or irregularities, indicates a long life and good health. Don't worry if your life line is short – look at the first phalange of the thumb; if this is long, it shows a will that is strong enough to overcome health problems.

2   **Head line:** the length of this is a guide to intelligence. The longer the line (and it can be anything from half the width of the hand to almost the full width) the more intelligent you are. If the line is high and straight, you are practical and realistic; if it slopes gently, you are imaginative and creative.

3   **Heart line:** a short, shallow, straight line suggests problems in showing affection. A line that is long and generously curved suggests a loving nature. Small lines radiating from the heart line suggest flirtations and affairs. A red heart line indicates a passionate nature, whereas a very pale line indicates indifference.

4   **Intuition line:** this line is not always present. If you have it, it denotes a high degree of intuitive insight.

5   **Sun line:** if this line starts at the base of the hand and ends in the Mount of Apollo, it denotes prosperity. Starting at the Mount of Venus, it shows artistic flair. If it starts at the head line, success will come in the middle years; starting at the heart line, it promises happiness in later life.

6   **Fate line:** if the line starts at the wrist and continues up to the Mount of Saturn, it indicates success as a reward for hard work. If the line starts at the Mount of Luna, it means you seek the recognition of others.

7   **Girdle of Venus:** if present, it suggests sensitivity and enthusiasm.

8   **Ambition line:** the point at which this line diverges from the life line shows how early or late in life your ambitions will be realised.

9   **Marriage lines:** the position of these lines is a guide to when you will marry – the closer to the heart line, the sooner it will be.

THE MOUNTS (see diagram) can be flat, well-rounded or highly developed.

A   **Venus:** flat, it indicates poor health; well-rounded, it is a sign of good health and a warm heart; highly-developed, it suggests a high sex-drive.

B   **Luna (moon):** flat, it indicates lack of imagination; well-rounded, it shows a love of travel and a sensitive, imaginative nature; highly developed, it can denote a strong, creative imagination, or over-sensitivity.

C   **Upper Mars:** if flat, you are easily led; well-rounded, it shows determination; highly developed, it suggests a quarrelsome nature.

D   **Neptune:** flat, it indicates communication problems; well-rounded, it shows an outgoing personality; highly developed, it denotes a good communicator.

E   **Jupiter:** flat, it suggests lack of ambition; well-rounded, it indicates self-confidence; highly developed, it shows a strong desire for power.

F   **Saturn:** flat, it indicates an orderly life; well-rounded, it shows a love of solitude; highly developed, it suggests antipathy towards other people.

G   **Apollo (sun):** a flat mount is a sign of a rather dull life and a lack of interest in culture; well-rounded, it indicates a cheerful nature and the ability to succeed at artistic or literary pursuits; highly developed, it can denote an ostentatious person, lacking in good taste.

H   **Mercury:** flat, it indicates gullibility; well-rounded, it denotes charm and quickness of thought; highly developed, it shows a materialistic streak.

J   **Lower Mars:** flat, it is a sign of cowardice; well-rounded, it indicates physical courage; highly developed, it shows fearlessness, but also cruelty.

flair: natural ability
gullibility: tendency to believe everything one is told
streak: a tendency in a person's character

When you read your palm you probably used the hand on which the lines are most marked. If you are under 35 this should normally be the left hand if you are right-handed, or the right hand if you are left-handed, for this is the hand that mirrors the qualities that you are born with. If you are over 35 the other hand should dominate for it is the hand that shows what you have done with these qualities.

2.2 Role-play: cross my palm with silver

Use the information you have learnt about the interpretation of palm lines to role-play a professional palm reading.

THE PALM READER

Describe your client's personality and predict his or her future. Give as precise details as you can.

CLIENT

Ask questions about your palm. Try to relate what the palm reader tells you to events in your life.

> *Useful language*
>
> Predicting the future:
>   You'll meet a tall dark stranger.
>   You won't be unhappy for long.
>   Ten years from now, you will be leading an interesting and creative life.
>   You will have overcome all the obstacles in your way by the time you are 40.
>   N.B. The present progressive tense is not usually used to predict the future.
>
> Talking about probability: (In these examples the chances of success get greater and greater.)
>   It looks as if you might succeed in your job.
>   You are likely to succeed.
>   You are bound to succeed.
>   *Or:* There is no likelihood of your succeeding.

2.3 Card fortune telling ☆

Here is one way of telling someone's fortune with a pack of cards.

Use a pack of 32 cards. If you only have an ordinary pack, remove the cards numbered 2–6. Shuffle well and cut with the left hand into 2 heaps (of equal or unequal size).
Put the top card of each pile to one side. These cards are called the Surprise.
Put the remaining cards into 1 pile and deal into 3 heaps of 10 cards each. These represent the past (left-hand heap), the present (centre) and the future (right-hand heap).
Spread the 10 cards of the first heap in a row from left to right.
Read off the meanings of the cards using the list given below. Some of the meanings will need interpreting!
Repeat the same process for the pile representing the present.
Repeat the same process for the pile representing the future.
Finally, consult the Surprise to see what unexpected event is going to influence your life and fortunes.

N.B. A *reversed* card is a card that is upside down. If you cannot tell this from your pack of cards because the printing is very regular you may have to mark one end with a pinprick or a dot.

HEART VALUES

Ace: Good news, a house, a love letter; *reversed*, disappointment, removal, or a friendly visit
King: Kind-hearted, loving man of fair complexion; *reversed*, an uncertain, inconstant lover
Queen: A generous loving woman, fair; *reversed*, crossed in love and capricious
Jack: A pleasure-loving bachelor, a friend or lover; *reversed*, a lover with a grievance
Ten: Good fortune and happiness; *reversed*, changes, a birth
Nine: Success, the wish card; *reversed*, passing troubles
Eight: Love, invitations, thoughts of marriage; *reversed*, unreciprocated affection, jealousy
Seven: Contentment and favours; *reversed*, boredom and jealousy

DIAMOND VALUES

Ace: Marriage offer, ring, bank notes; *reversed*, demand for debt, bad news
King: Fair or grey-haired man, widower; *reversed*, treachery and deceit
Queen: Fair woman, widow, a gossip; *reversed*, untrustworthy, a flirt
Jack: An official, a messenger; *reversed*, mischief-maker
Ten: Journey or removal, finance; *reversed*, misfortune
Nine: Anxiety, news; *reversed*, danger, family quarrels
Eight: Amorous, short journey; *reversed*, affections ignored
Seven: Child, unfriendly criticism; *reversed*, scandal, minor successes

CLUB VALUES

Ace: Good luck, papers or letters bringing in money, or good news; *reversed*, ill news, delayed letter
King: A dark man, friendly and straight; *reversed*, worries and slight troubles
Queen: Dark woman, affectionate; *reversed*, undependable, perplexities
Jack: Athlete, clever, good lover; *reversed*, luck may change
Ten: Ease and prosperity, journey, luck; *reversed*, sea voyage, estrangement
Nine: Legacy; *reversed*, obstacles
Eight: The love of a dark man or woman, joy and good luck in consequence; *reversed*, documents causing trouble, litigation
Seven: Success with money; *reversed*, financial worries and losses

SPADE VALUES

Ace: Satisfaction in love, high building; *reversed*, sorrow, death, disappointments

King: Widower, untrustworthy lawyer; *reversed*, a very dangerous enemy, impending evil

Queen: Widow, faithful friend; *reversed*, intrigue, treacherous woman

Jack: Doctor or barrister, bad mannered; *reversed*, deceitful, traitor

Ten: Long journey, grief; *reversed*, slight sickness

Nine: Failure, financial or domestic; *reversed*, death of dear friend

Eight: Impending illness, sorrow; *reversed*, rejected affection, evil living, quarrels

Seven: A change for the worse, a resolution; *reversed*, accidents or losses

ill news: a more usual expression is bad news

2.4 Discussion

What other forms of fortune telling do you know of?

Has any one in the class ever had his or her fortune told professionally? Did it come true?

Are any forms of fortune telling more reliable than others?

Are they all a hoax? If so, why does the press pay so much attention to them?

3 How honest are you?

3.1 ☆

HOW HONEST ARE YOU, REALLY? TEST YOURSELF!

This provocative quiz may provide some surprises. Answer each question as candidly as possible. (Assume in every case that you wouldn't be caught in any wrongdoing; being honest for fear of retribution doesn't count.) Following the test are instructions for scoring.

1 You find a wallet containing nearly $1,000, plus identification. Do you keep the cash?
   No ( )   Maybe ( )   Yes ( )

2 You want to add a garage to your house, but a building inspector says the structure will violate a zoning ordinance. He later hints, however, that for $100 he will okay the construction anyway. Do you give him the money?
   No ( )   Maybe ( )   Yes ( )

3 You sell your house to a woman who, for reasons of her own, pays you in cash. By reporting only part of this payment to the IRS, and putting the rest in a bank vault, you can save thousands. Do you?
   No ( )   Maybe ( )   Yes ( )

4 A catalog store ships you a $500 television, but bills you only for a $25 TV-table. Do you quietly send a check for the smaller sum?
   No ( )   Maybe ( )   Yes ( )

5 Checking in at a fine hotel, you find a thick, new bathmat in exactly the color you need. Before you leave, you could hide it in your suitcase. Do you?
   No ( )   Maybe ( )   Yes ( )

6 You have dinner with a colleague in an expensive restaurant. Paying the bill, she hands you the receipt and says, "Tell your company you took *me* to dinner—make yourself fifty bucks." Do you?
   No ( )   Maybe ( )   Yes ( )

7 In the ladies' room of a hotel's restaurant, you take off your wedding band, then forget to put it back on. By the time you return to the ladies' room for the ring, it's gone. Your insurance doesn't cover this kind of loss, but if you claim the ring was stolen from your hotel room, you could be reimbursed. Do you lie to your insurance company?
   No ( )   Maybe ( )   Yes ( )

8 Late for an evening engagement, you speed through a stop sign and dent an oncoming car. This accident could cost you your license, so to make the judge more lenient, you propose to tell him that, though you were driving carefully, you were blinded by the other vehicle's oncoming lights. Do you tell this story to the judge, and lie under oath?
   No ( )   Maybe ( )   Yes ( )

9 Your car is for sale, and someone agrees to pay the price you name—he gives you a deposit and the two of you shake hands. Later on, another customer offers you $200 more. She urges you to tell the first customer you've changed your mind and send him back his deposit. Do you?
   No ( )   Maybe ( )   Yes ( )

Scoring: *Give yourself two points for each No, one point for each Maybe and no points for each Yes. Then add up and see how your honesty rates. 18: You're a straight arrow, perfect. 12 to 17: Your honesty is laudable. 7 to 11: Your honesty is rather selective, or—depending on how you look at it—shaky. 1 to 6: You're a self-seeker with a few leftover qualms. 0: You look out only for Number One; you're a thorough cheat.*

a zoning ordinance: an order, usually from a local government authority, dictating where buildings can be constructed
IRS: Inland Revenue Services, organisation responsible for collecting taxes
to bill: (Am.) to send a bill

3.2 Honest geography

Honesty is very often a relative concept and depends on conventions in different societies. For instance, bribery is considered very bad in some countries whereas in others it is almost institutionalised. Stealing is considered a greater or lesser crime depending on where you live, and some people say that the dishonesty of a politician like Richard Nixon would not have brought about his downfall in any other country but the United States of America. On the world map below pin-point any parts of the globe that you know of that have particularly honest or dishonest principles. Work with a partner.

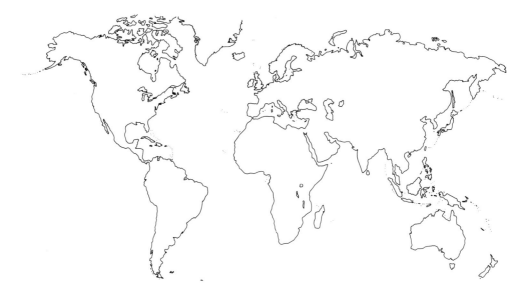

Useful language

incorruptible	bribery, corruption
trustworthy	untrustworthy
scrupulous	unscrupulous
	a lie, a fib
	a confidence trick
to be reliable	to trick
to have principles	to double cross
to be upright	to fiddle
	to swindle

to have something on one's conscience
to give someone the benefit of the doubt

3.3 White lies

A white lie is a lie that is considered to be justified, or even praiseworthy, if it is in the interests of the person or people to whom it is told. For example, to avoid offending someone, you might invent a reason for not accepting an invitation to a party that you don't want to go to, or you might admire a friend's new clothes when in fact you think they are frightful. Work with a partner.

a) Compile a list of situations in which you think a white lie would be justified.
b) Recall occasions on which you have told a white lie and explain why it was justified.

3.4 More or less honest

Is there a scale of dishonesty? Make a list of dishonest acts and consider whether they are all equally bad for you or if some are worse than others. Compare your list with somebody else's.

Useful language

Classifying activities:
   omitting certain bits of income on a tax return
   reading other people's letters
   buying a dissertation to obtain an academic qualification
   cheating at cards
   cheating in an exam
   shoplifting small items
   claiming more than you spent on an expense account
   turning the milometer back when selling a car
   travelling on the underground without a ticket
   taking home stationery from the office

3.5 Tell me a tale

a) Work in groups of five or six. Each member of the group tells a story that is either completely true or completely false. The other members of the group must decide whether they think the story is true or not.
b) Work in groups of three. Choose an incident that happened to one of you (a meeting with a famous person, an unusual event, an exciting occasion). Prepare three versions of the story, the real one and two fake ones. Each person tells their version to the rest of the class which must decide who is telling the truth.

How often were you right? What criteria were you basing your judgements on?

3.6 Role-play: the truth is hard to tell

Sometimes the truth is difficult to tell and sounds better if embellished. Pick one of the following situations and build up a short scene, trying to make the truth sound less unpleasant than it is. You will need a few minutes to decide on your strategy: hedging, rapidly changing the subject, presenting other advantages, making promises and so on. The person on the receiving end will also need to decide on his or her attitude.

A student announces his or her failure of exams for the second time running to a not-so-understanding parent.

A husband or wife returns home late from work for the third time in a week to be greeted by a suspicious spouse.

You had agreed to go on holiday with a friend. At the last minute you decide not to go. You break the news to your friend, knowing that you have probably ruined his or her holiday.

You have promised to pay back some money you borrowed from a friend by a certain date. You know he or she needs the money but you cannot honour your promise.

Useful language

Apologising, hedging:

Look at the language used in this one-sided telephone conversation.

Hello, Mary, this is Dick. Look, you know that weekend we planned in Venice? Well, um, you see, it's like this, I'm afraid I can't make it.

.....

No, really, I'm terribly sorry but I can't come after all.

.....

I'm frightfully sorry, honestly, but something has come up at work and the boss is putting the pressure on.

.....

Anyway, we weren't absolutely set on going this weekend, were we? And in any case I'm a bit broke at the moment. Besides, it will be so much warmer if we go in the spring.

.....

And by the way, the boss is promising a rise in salary, a kind of promotion or something, if I get a few new contracts.

.....

I promise I'll make it up to you, I really will.

3.7 Surprise quiz ☆

Answer these questions. Work by yourself. You will find out what the object of the test is — and what it has to do with honesty — when you come to look at the answers.

DIRECTIONS If on the whole you agree with a statement, check TRUE. If you disagree with a statement, or consider it doubtful, check FALSE.

1. Sometimes anger makes you do things you would not do otherwise .... TRUE ☐ FALSE ☐

2. If someone cheats you, you never let him get away with it .... TRUE ☐ FALSE ☐

3. When someone smokes illegally in a theatre or train, you usually see to it that he is stopped .... TRUE ☐ FALSE ☐

4. You have never violated any of the laws of your community .... TRUE ☐ FALSE ☐

5. Usually you tend to avoid people who do not like you .... TRUE ☐ FALSE ☐

6. You sometimes read comics, detective stories or other 'low-brow' writing with enjoyment .... TRUE ☐ FALSE ☐

7. You are not inclined to like people simply because they like you .... TRUE ☐ FALSE ☐

8. When people are less fortunate than yourself, you usually do something to help them .... TRUE ☐ FALSE ☐

9. Being interested in literature, you manage to read most of the good books published each year .... TRUE ☐ FALSE ☐

10. You are inclined to dislike a person when that person dislikes you .... TRUE ☐ FALSE ☐

11. Sometimes you feel a bit 'blue' or depressed .... TRUE ☐ FALSE ☐

12. You have at least some idea of the meaning of the word PRETORATORY .... TRUE ☐ FALSE ☐

13. On occasion you have seized a choice tit-bit at dinner, although you knew somebody else might have wanted it .... TRUE ☐ FALSE ☐

14. At times you pretend to know more than you do .... TRUE ☐ FALSE ☐

15. When going to the movies with friends, you sometimes want them to attend a picture you prefer rather than one which they prefer .... TRUE ☐ FALSE ☐

Now check your score on page 99.

What this test means

If this test were to be marked by someone other than yourself, a low score could be interpreted to mean that you make a habit of 'lying to win approval' – a common social fault.

Since you do all the marking and are your own judge, however, a low score here would more likely signify that you often lie to yourself. Conversely, a high score would probably mean that you are inclined to face issues squarely instead of 'kidding yourself'.

3.8 Letter writing ☆

Advertising is one area in which there is often a great deal of dishonesty. In Great Britain there exists an Advertising Standards Authority to which you can write and complain about false claims in advertising. Look at the advertisement below and the letters complaining about it. Write a similar letter about a dishonest advertisement that you know of.

```
                                              20 Cowford Drive
                                              Little Windlesmere
                                              Hampshire
The Director                                  15th May 1983
The Advertising Standards Board
1 Bruton Way
London W.1.

Dear Sir,

I should like to point out an advertisement that has recently appeared in the
national press. It is for a slimming product named 'Slimsticks'. I have not tried
out the efficiency of the product, having no need for such gimmicks myself.
However, I wish to complain about the blatant dishonesty of the advertisement. The
photographs of the 'lady' before and after taking the product have obviously been
tampered with by the photographer.

The question I would like to raise is whether it is morally right to raise our
young women's hopes of achieving a trim figure through trick photography.
Personally, I feel that this should not be allowed and hope that you will do your
utmost to stop such an outrage.

              Yours faithfully,
              Arnold Blinks
              Lt. Col. Arnold Blinks
```

12, Seaview Terrace,
Southdown,
Essex.

The Director,
The Advertising Standards Board,
1, Bruton Way,
London, W.1.

15th. July 1983.

Dear Sir, I am writing to complain about a scandalous advertisement that has recently appeared in my weekly magazine, Women's Wonders. I bought the product advertised, Slimsticks, and followed the instructions exactly. After four weeks I am still the same weight.

I am sending you a copy of this advertisement so that such outrageous dishonesty can be stopped.

Yours faithfully,
Mabel Marshall.

3.9 Discussion

Is being honest dull? Are honest people dull?
What forms of professional dishonesty do you know of that are common practice among doctors, lawyers, etc.? What about the world of commerce?
Do all children steal at some stage? How should they be treated when they do?
Are lie detectors morally acceptable in the fight against crime?
Is it ever acceptable to use torture to obtain the truth from someone?

4 Food and fitness

4.1 Fighting fit ☆

How much do you know about keeping fit? Do this quiz with a partner. Read the following statements and say whether they are true or false.

1. If you take more exercise, your appetite will increase and keep you from losing weight.
2. Exercise changes fat into muscle.
3. A good way to lose weight is to take exercise which makes you sweat heavily.
4. Vitamin pills can give an extra burst of energy.
5. Physical exercise is not necessary for losing weight. Dieting alone is enough.
6. To burn up the calories contained in a 4 oz (approx. 110 g) bar of chocolate you must walk for over 2 hours at 4 m.p.h. (approx. 6.5 km.p.h.).
7. A high protein, low carbohydrate diet is ideal for losing weight.
8. People who do not eat meat, fish or poultry are not as healthy as those who do.
9. When dieting you should avoid starchy foods such as bread and potatoes.
10. Eating between meals is bad for you.
11. A large lunch will not cause you to put on as much weight as a meal of the same size eaten in the evening.
12. If your diet is varied you must be getting proper nourishment.
13. A glass of wine or a glass of scotch will help you sleep well.
14. Most people need eight or nine hours of sleep a night.
15. Sleeping less than five hours a night shortens your life expectancy.
16. Laughter helps you keep fit.

You will find the answers on page 99.

How did you score?

If you answered all 16 questions right, you know all about keeping fit. If you have more than 12 right answers you have quite a good idea about keeping yourself in top shape. If you have less than 12 right answers you are the victim of quite a few common misconceptions and may well not be as fit as you could be.

4.2 Is this your problem? ☆

Can you write out the instructions for the exercises that this lady is trying to do? She gives up rather too soon. Try to build the exercise programme into a possible ten-minute daily routine. Can you try it out on someone?

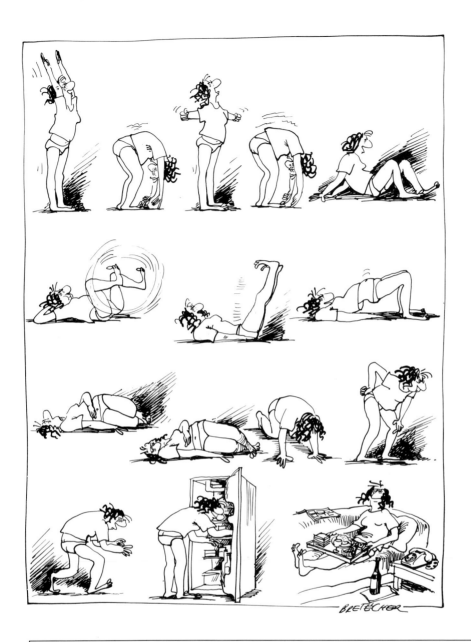

Useful language		
feet apart	to stretch your arms	stomach
feet together	to bend	chest, bust
off the ground	to raise	trunk
from side to side	to lift	waist
towards the ceiling	to roll	hips
sideways	to straighten	spine
backwards, forwards		buttocks, behind, bottom
on all fours		thighs
		shoulders

4.3 Overweight? Underweight? ☆

Work out your ideal weight from the chart below. Compare the size of your hands and feet and the breadth of your shoulders with other people to see if you have a large, medium or small frame.

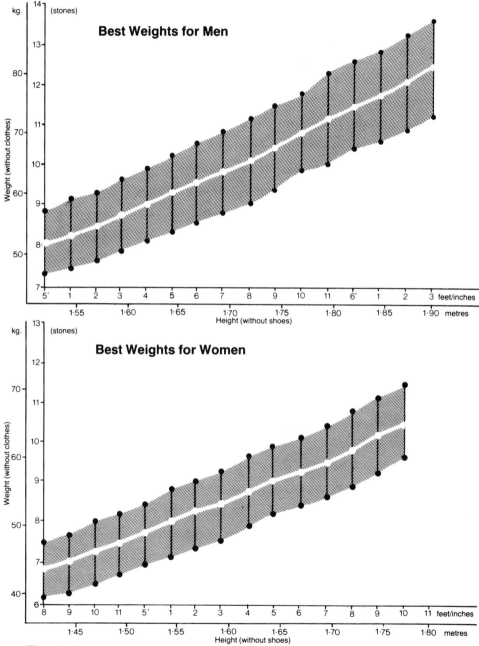

The shaded areas show the range of best or desirable weights, allowing for differences in sizes of body frames – large, average or small – for each height.

4.4 A calorie count down ☆

Using the table below, calculate how many calories you have consumed in the last 24 hours. Compare results with a partner.

Type of food	Calories per 100g (approx. 3.5oz) (unless other quantity stated)	Type of food	Calories per 100g (approx. 3.5oz) (unless other quantity stated)
Cereals and cereal foods		Lamb (lean only)	125
Bread (white, 4 slices)	243	Liver	130
Bread (wholemeal, 4 slices)	228	Pork	260
Cornflakes	367	Rabbit	150
Flour	350	Sausage	350
Macaroni	114	Sweetbreads	120
Rice	122	Tongue	200
		Tripe	102
		Turkey	130
Milk products and eggs		Veal	125
Butter	770	Venison	175
Cheese (Camembert)	260		
Cheese (Cheddar, Cheshire, Gorgonzola, Stilton, etc.)	400	**Fats and oils**	
Cream	300	Lard	920
Eggs (2 largish eggs)	160	Margarine	795
Milk (fresh, skimmed)	35	Olive oil	930
Milk (fresh, whole)	66		
Yoghurt (low fat)	54	**Fish**	
		Caviar	350
Meat, poultry and game		Cod	100
Bacon	405	Crab	127
Beef (lean only)	165	Haddock	100
Beef (lean and fat)	200	Halibut	137
Brain (calf)	103	Herring	150
Chicken (without skin)	100-150	Lobster	80
Duck (with skin)	330	Mackerel	150
Duck (without skin)	160	Mussels	87
Ham (2 average slices)	260	Oysters	50
Hare	195	Plaice	100
Heart (sheep)	239	Prawns	104
Kidney	100	Salmon	200
Lamb (lean and fat)	260		⟫→

Type of food	Calories per 100g (approx. 3.5oz) (unless other quantity stated)
Sardines (fresh)	180
Sardines (tinned)	294
Shrimps	114
Sole	100
Trout	80
Turbot	70
Vegetables	
Artichokes	15
Asparagus	18
Beans (French or runner)	7
Beans (haricot)	90
Beetroot	44
Cabbage	20
Carrots	22
Cauliflower	11
Celery	9
Cucumber	9
Leeks	25
Lentils	95
Lettuce	11
Mushrooms	10
Peas	50
Potatoes	80
Potato chips	239
Potato crisps	559
Spinach	26
Tomatoes	14
Fruit and nuts	
Apples	50
Apricots	28
Apricots (canned in syrup)	106
Apricots (dried)	183
Avocado pears	90
Bananas	80
Cherries	47
Dates	248
Grapes	63
Grapefruit	22
Melon	24
Olives	126
Oranges	35
Peaches	37
Pears	40
Pineapple	46
Plums	38
Raisins (dried)	247
Raspberries	25
Strawberries	26
Almonds	598
Chestnuts	172
Peanuts	603
Walnuts	549
Puddings, cakes, sweets, etc.	
Apple pie	190
Biscuits (plain)	435
Cake (fruit)	378
Cake (plain)	308
Chocolate	550
Honey	288
Ice cream	196
Jam	260
Jelly	82
Rice pudding	144
Sugar	395
Sweets	380
Trifle	150
Beverages	
Beer	30
Champagne	74
Cider	37
Cocoa powder	452
Spirits (70% proof)	222
Wines (dry white)	75
Wines (Martini, port)	156
Wines (red table)	68
Wines (sweet white)	93

4.5 What the average body burns ☆

Check your result against this table which shows how many calories a day the average man or woman burns. Your own personal needs will depend on your build and your body chemistry.

Age	Women	Men
16	2,300	2,900
25	2,200 – 2,700	2,700 – 3,600
45	2,200 – 2,500	2,600 – 2,900
65	2,200 or less	about 2,500

4.6 Diet menus ☆

Using the calorie table, design two sets of menus for a week, one for a friend who is trying to slim and one for a friend who is trying to put on weight.

4.7 Role-play: keeping fit

Work in pairs on this radio interview.

PAUL(A) SHAPE, AUTHOR

You have just written a best-seller on how to keep fit. You are anxious to dispel some popular misconceptions about the subject.

PAT AMBLE, JOURNALIST AND RADIO PERSONALITY

You are interviewing Paul(a) Shape on your weekend magazine programme about his / her recent best-seller on how to keep fit. You do not agree with all his / her theories.

Useful language

Making comparisons:
  People need less sleep than they think.
  The older people get, the more they worry about having enough sleep.
  The more they worry, the less they sleep.
  The sooner they stop worrying, the sooner they will relax and enjoy life.
  The more we exercise, the healthier we are.
  Rather than eat a well-balanced diet, people often prefer just to eat red meat.

Polite disagreement:
  Don't you think that you are going a little too far when you say ...?
  Haven't you exaggerated a little in claiming ...?
  Wouldn't you say that ...?
  Surely violent exercise is very bad for the heart?
  Don't you really mean that ...?

4.8 Life expectancy ☆

We have seen that the amount you do or do not sleep can affect your life expectancy. So can being overweight, but so can many other things. Work out your life expectancy from the table below. You will find the average life expectancy for someone your age in the column on the left. To this figure you add on or take away the totals in the columns on the right.

Age	Life Expect.	If you are a woman add 3 years to your life expectancy	Add	Take away	Your score
15	70.7				
16	70.8	For each of your grandparents			
17	70.8	who lived to 80 or more	1		
18	70.9				
19	71	Your mother lived to more than 80	4		
20	71.1	Your father lived to more than 80	2		
21	71.1				
22	71.2				
23	71.3	A brother, sister or parent died of			
24	71.3	a heart attack, a stroke or			
25	71.4	arteriosclerosis before 50		4	
26	71.5	Between 50 and 60		2	
27	71.6				
28	71.6				
29	71.7				
30	71.8	They died of diabetes before 60		3	
31	71.8	They died of stomach cancer before 60		2	
32	71.9				
33	72				
34	72	You smoke per day: more than 40 cigarettes		12	
35	72.1	between 20 and 40		7	
36	72.2	less than 20		2	
37	72.2				
38	72.3				
39	72.4	You like to have sexual relations			
40	72.5	at least once or twice a week	2		
41	72.6				
42	72.7				
43	72.8	You have a complete medical			
44	72.9	check-up at least once a year	2		
45	73				
46	73.2				
47	73.3	You are overweight		2	
48	73.5				
49	73.6	You sleep more than 10 hours a night			
50	73.8	or less than 5		2	
51	74				
52	74.2				
53	74.4	You are a moderate drinker			
54	74.7	(1 or 2 whiskies or ½ litre wine			
55	74.9	or 4 glasses beer a day)	3		
56	75.1	You do not drink	0		
57	75.4	You drink a lot		8	
58	75.7				
59	76				
60	76.3				
61	76.6	You take exercise 3 times a week: cycling,			
62	77	fast walking, swimming, dancing	3		
63	77.3				
64	77.7				
65	78.1	You are a university graduate,			
66	78.4	a lawyer, a doctor	3		
67	78.9	You have passed G.C.E. 'A' levels	2		
68	79.3				
69	79.7				
70	80.2	You live in a town		1	
71	80.7	You live in the country	1		
72	81.2				
73	81.7				
74	82.2	You are married or live with someone	1		
75	82.8	You live alone		9	
76	83.3	You are a widower		7	
77	83.9	A woman living alone (separated or divorced)		4	
78	84.5	Widow		3½	
79	85.1				
80	85.7				

university graduate: someone who has successfully completed a 3 or 4 year course at university

G.C.E. 'A' level: a school-leaving exam in Britain, taken at about 18

4.9 Discussion

What diets, if any, have you followed? Did they work?
Do you know of any special diets that guarantee success?
Is it better to be too fat or too thin? Is our society too obsessed with problems of weight and fitness?
Do men worry about weight as much as women?
Does the way the western world eats have any effect on world food problems?
Do people follow diets for reasons other than fitness and health? Do you know of any such diets?

5 Life's tensions

5.1 How stress-proof are you? ☆

Study the following situations and consider what your reaction would be in each of them. If you think you would have any of the reactions listed beneath each situation, place a tick in the box beside it.

Example
You have been invited to dinner with your boss to meet some very important business contacts. During the meal you knock over an almost full bottle of wine. Would you blush? Would you stammer? If so, fill in the boxes as in the example. Would you:

feel embarrassed? ☐   feel calm?   ☐
blush?   ✓   feel amused?   ☐
stammer?   ✓   be indifferent? ☐

You may sometimes find yourself ticking columns on the left and the right. For example, you might feel embarrassed but calm in the situation above.

---

1 You have driven through some traffic lights as they were turning red. You are stopped by a policeman who senses that you are in a hurry and seems to be taking his time deliberately. Do you:

feel uneasy?   ☐   behave in a friendly manner? ☐
start perspiring?   ☐   act coolly?   ☐
behave aggressively?   ☐   look detached?   ☐

2 At a friend's wedding you are unexpectedly asked to make a speech. Do you:

blush?   ☐   feel amused?   ☐
feel your hands trembling? ☐   feel composed?   ☐
begin to stutter nervously? ☐   feel pleased and flattered?   ☐

3 You have just finished dining in a restaurant and have asked the waiter for the bill. You suddenly discover that you have left both your wallet and your cheque book at home. Do you:

feel embarrassed?   ☐   remain calm?   ☐
start stammering?   ☐   simply tell the waiter what has
have a nervous laugh? ☐   happened?   ☐
                             have a natural laugh?   ☐

4 You are caught travelling on a bus without a ticket. Your reaction is:

a feeling of shame? ☐	a feeling of indifference? ☐
a forced smile? ☐	an amused smile? ☐
a shortness of breath? ☐	a look of imperturbability? ☐

5 Travelling down the motorway at 70 m.p.h. (approx. 113 km.p.h.) you have a flat tyre. You manage to stop on the hard shoulder. Do you:

feel rage? ☐	remain unflappable? ☐
feel at a complete loss? ☐	feel quite able to cope with the situation? ☐
become exasperated? ☐	reflect calmly on what to do next? ☐

6 You are caught between floors in a lift. You are alone. Do you:

get damp palms? ☐	keep your composure? ☐
grow pale? ☐	feel not particularly worried? ☐
panic? ☐	wait patiently to be rescued? ☐

7 You are returning from a holiday abroad and have more cigarettes and spirits in your suitcase than are permitted by the regulations. A customs officer asks you to open your suitcase. Do you:

get worked up and agitated? ☐	keep your self-control? ☐
feel afraid? ☐	behave with resignation? ☐
find your hands trembling? ☐	consider that you have lost this round in a fair game? ☐

8 At a party you meet someone who greets you very warmly as an old friend, but you cannot remember his name, or even where you have met him before. Do you react:

with embarrassed self-consciousness? ☐	by bluffing your way out of the situation? ☐
with anxiety? ☐	by honestly avowing the inadequacy of your memory? ☐
with a sinking feeling in your stomach? ☐	by laughing the matter off? ☐

9 You are walking out of a department store when you suddenly realise you are clutching an article that you have forgotten to pay for. You see someone who looks as if he might be the store detective looming up. Do you:

lose your sang-froid? ☐	behave in a friendly manner? ☐
wish the ground would open up and swallow you? ☐	remain completely unruffled? ☐
have palpitations? ☐	act nonchalantly? ☐

⟫→

How to score

The maximum score for this quiz is 52 points. Score one point for every possibility you have *not* ticked (i.e. blank boxes) in the left-hand columns and one point for every possibility you *have* ticked in the right-hand columns. Now check your resilience to stress in the chart below.

Age	14–16	17–21	22–30	30+	Resilience to stress
Points	46–52	47–52	48–52	50–52	Very strong. You are extremely stress proof and it is almost impossible to embarrass you. The worst will have to come to the worst before you get upset.
	42–45	43–46	44–47	45–49	Strong. You are an imperturbable character who does not often lose calm and composure. Though you may occasionally give way to your feelings, you are seldom embarrassed.
	32–41	33–42	34–43	35–44	Average to strong. Your ability to cope with situations of stress is within the upper half of the normal range.
	21–40	23–32	23–33	23–34	Average to weak. Although your resilience to stress is within the normal range, you tend to get worked up quite easily and on occasion lose your equanimity.
	0–20	0–22	0–22	0–22	Weak. You need to develop strategies to cope with the uneasiness and embarrassment you feel in difficult situations. Try to react with a sense of humour and adopt a calm and collected attitude.

5.2 Is life getting you down? ☆

The minor mishaps described in the quiz above are not the only source of stress in our lives. A lot is caused by small irritations in our daily existence. With a partner, make a list of everything that has irritated you both over the past year. Your list may include such things as the noise the neighbours make, the fact that you are slightly overweight or that your new shoes hurt!

5.3 Role-play: taking it easy

Work with a partner.

These are typical scenes from the life of Mr Jim Rusher.

You and your partner are colleagues of Mr Rusher's, but you live much less hectic lives. You are worried about your colleague who has been more and more nervy and irritable lately. Over a cup of coffee you are discussing ways in which he could make his life more relaxed. You can begin: 'I'm very worried about Jim ...'.

> *Useful language*
> Making suggestions:
>   Why doesn't he try to relax more?
>   He should try and get away from it all.
>   He really ought to take things more easily.
>   Unless he stops worrying, he might even have a heart attack.
>   If I were him, I'd take a good long holiday.
>   He'd better find some other interest outside his work.

5.4 Job stress ☆

Such things as our general living conditions, our way of life, whether we live in a town or in the country, etc. affect the amount of stress we suffer. However, the biggest single influence on stress is, very often, the job we do.

With a partner, arrange this list of jobs and professions in the order of their stress potential. Add to the list any two particularly stressful or unstressful jobs that you know of.

a farmer on a small mountain farm
a long-distance lorry driver
a housewife, mother of three children
a managing director
a politician
a teacher in a secondary school
a university professor
a lawyer
a bar tender in a pub
a writer
an actor
a journalist
a miner
a road-worker working with a pneumatic drill
a gardener
a train-driver
a fireman
a travelling salesman
a worker on the production line in a factory
a taxi driver in a large town

5.5 Major life events ☆

Major life events also contribute to the stress in our lives. This type of stress can be measured on Dr Rahe's scale. With a partner, work through this scale and calculate your scores.

1.	Death of spouse	100
2.	Divorce	73
3.	Marital separation	65
4.	Jail term	63
5.	Death of close family member	63
6.	Personal injury or illness	53
7.	Marriage	50
8.	Fired at work	47
9.	Marital reconciliation	45
10.	Retirement	45
11.	Change in health of family member	44
12.	Pregnancy	40
13.	Sex difficulties	39
14.	Gain of new family member	39
15.	Business readjustment	39
16.	Change in financial state	38
17.	Death of close friend	37
18.	Change to different line of work	36
19.	Change in number of arguments with spouse	35
20.	A large mortgage or loan	31
21.	Foreclosure of mortgage or loan	30

22.	Change in responsibilities at work	29
23.	Son or daughter leaving home	29
24.	Trouble with in-laws	29
25.	Outstanding personal achievement	28
26.	Spouse begins or stops work	26
27.	Begin or end school or college	26
28.	Change in living conditions	25
29.	A change in personal habits	24
30.	Trouble with the boss	23
31.	Change in work hours or conditions	20
32.	Change in residence	20
33.	Change in school or college	20
34.	Change in recreation	19
35.	Change in church activities	19
36.	Change in social activities	18
37.	A moderate mortgage or loan	17
38.	Change in sleeping habits	16
39.	Change in number of family get-togethers	15
40.	Change in eating habits	15
41.	Holiday	13
42.	Christmas	12
43.	Minor violations of the law	11

What it means

Below 60: Your life has been unusually free from stress lately.

60 to 80: You have had a normal amount of stress recently. This score is average for the ordinary wear and tear of life.

80 to 100: The stress in your life is a little high, probably because of one recent event.

100 upwards: Pressures are piling up, either at home or work, or both. You are under serious stress, and the higher you score above 100 the worse the strain.

Useful language

Talking about the recent past:
  Have you just got married?
  Have you retired recently?

If you are talking about events that are of a continuous or repetitive nature you can ask questions like this:
  Have you been sleeping less lately?
  Have you been seeing more of your family?
  Have you been eating more recently?
  Have you been having trouble with your in-laws?

If you are almost sure that the answer to your question is no, you can ask questions like this:
  Your wife isn't expecting a baby, is she?
  You haven't changed your job lately, have you?
  You haven't moved house in the last six months, have you?

6 A taste of taste

6.1 Good taste ☆

Taste is often a question of culture or of fashion. However, the aspects of artistic composition tested in this set of schematic drawings are rather more universal. Unity of form, balance, rhythm and so on are elements that have stood the test of time and are more or less generally agreed upon.

Part 1: Decide which sketch in each row best illustrates the word at the left of that row. Discuss your choice with a partner before looking at the answers on page 100.

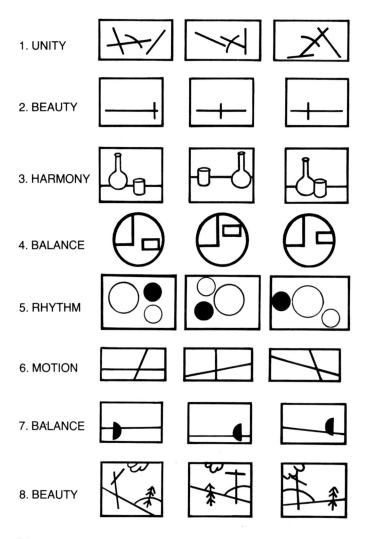

1. UNITY
2. BEAUTY
3. HARMONY
4. BALANCE
5. RHYTHM
6. MOTION
7. BALANCE
8. BEAUTY

9. GRACE

10. POISE

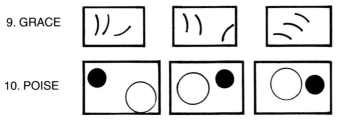

Part 2: This part of the test is more to do with cultural norms and fashions in taste.

Decide which phrase is the best answer to the question, or which best completes the statement. Work with a partner. Discuss your choice before looking at the answers on page 100.

---

1. Joe Doe is 5 feet 4 inches tall and weighs 200 pounds, which makes him a pretty plump person by any standard. Which pattern do you recommend for his suit?

    a. Large over-all plaid ☐
    b. Faint pin-stripe ☐
    c. Strong, well-spaced vertical stripes ☐

2. Select the best fit for the same Mr. Doe's suits.

    a. Loose, easy drape ☐
    b. Neither loose nor form-fitting ☐
    c. Form-fitting ☐

3. Can it be in good taste to place a *modern* chair and sofa in a room which contains "period" furniture?

    a. Yes ☐
    b. No ☐

4. Suppose you have a long room full of color and with drapes bearing a large floral design. Would you try to match this with a colorful carpet also of floral design, or would you select a carpet neutral in color and inconspicuous in design?

    a. Colour ☐
    b. Neutral ☐

5. The real function of a painter is not so much just to paint, but rather to "hold a mirror up to nature"; that is, to reproduce a given object as faithfully as possible.

    a. Yes ☐
    b. No ☐

6. In their dress, people should be quick to adopt the latest fashions – if they have the price.

  a. Yes ☐
  b. No ☐

7. A structure will always be in good taste if it is patterned after a classic example of architectural excellence, such as a Greek temple or a Gothic church.

  a. Yes ☐
  b. No ☐

8. Large furniture in a small room will make the room appear larger.

  a. Yes ☐
  b. No ☐
  c. Sometimes ☐

9. Small women look better in waist-length jackets than do tall women.

  a. Yes ☐
  b. No ☐
  c. Yes, if the jacket is of chinchilla ☐

10. Pictures of different sizes and shapes generally look better when hung–

  a. With the *tops* of the frames on one level ☐
  b. With the *bottoms* of the frames on one level ☐

---

drapes: (Am.) curtains
chinchilla: a type of animal fur

What your score means

Average Score: 28

Excellent	(upper ten per cent) 39–50
Good	(next twenty-five per cent) 33–38
Fair	(next thirty-five per cent) 26–32
Inferior	(low thirty per cent) 0–25

6.2 Flair ☆

Taste can very often be observed in the way people dress. The kind of person who always seems to have just the right clothes, clothes that suit both him or herself and the occasion, is said to have flair. Think of someone you know who has this quality (or who is totally without it) and describe him / her to your partner. Try and analyse just what the quality is through describing particular examples.

> *Useful language*
>
> clothes sense   fussy
> flawless taste   shabby
> fastidious   smart
> vulgar   stylish
> flashy   fashionable
> cheap
>
> Describing people. Physical appearance:
>   What a well-dressed / badly-dressed woman!
>   He's a very elegant man.
>   The way she walks is so inelegant.
>   She always wears such suitable / unsuitable clothes.
>   Her way of dressing is completely tasteless.
>   She's very graceful.
>
> Describing people. Behaviour:
>   She's a very well-mannered / ill-mannered person.
>   He's extremely polite / impolite.
>   He's so courteous / discourteous.

6.3 The top ten

Work with a partner. Choose a set of people (politicians, the international set, famous wives, etc.). Make a list of the ten best-dressed men or the ten best-dressed women. Compare your list with the other lists in the class. Alternatively, make a list of the ten least well-dressed men or women.

6.4 Around the house

Although there may be some basic rules as to what constitutes good taste, there are also a lot of varieties of taste. People talk about classical taste, old-fashioned taste, modern taste, exotic taste, eccentric taste and so on. The way people decorate their houses very often reflects their type of taste. Find a photograph or a picture of an interior in which you recognise a taste that is radically different from your own personal or national style. Why is it different? What do you like or dislike about it? Explain your feelings in detail to a partner. Be precise.

6.5 The rules of good taste

Work in groups of four or five. Can you agree on a set of five basic rules of good taste:

a) for decorating a house?
b) for how to dress?

Compare your list with the criteria of other groups.

6.6 Colours

Does everyone react to colour in the same way? Do preferences for one colour or another reflect a person's psychological make-up? Does the value attributed to colour simply reflect cultural rules? Try one of these simple experiments and see if you can reach any conclusions. Work in groups of four or five.

a) Each group makes a set of coloured cards: grey, blue, green, red, yellow, violet, brown, black. Lay the cards out one by one. Each person describes the feelings that the colour arouses in him or her. Contrasts between the colours and combinations can also be discussed.
b) Each group collects a set of postcard reproductions of paintings, each with a strong single colour element. The cards are circulated round the group. Each student notes down his or her reactions to the colours in the paintings, ignoring for the moment the compositional or thematic elements of the painting. There is no discussion at this stage. When all the cards have been examined by every member of the group, impressions are compared. The relationship between the colours and the themes of the paintings can also be examined.

6.7 Role-play: the interior decorator

THE CLIENT

You want to redecorate your house / flat. You are discussing the problem with an interior decorator. You describe your living accommodation as it is at the moment, its advantages and disadvantages and what you would like to change. You have some quite definite ideas yourself and you are a little worried that the interior decorator's suggestions are too wild for you and may go out of fashion quickly. You do not think that his suggestions about colour schemes take your own personality and taste into account.

THE INTERIOR DECORATOR

You are seeing a client about redecorating his home. You listen to his or her ideas but try to impress him or her with your own modern and daring conceptions of design. You have, for example, very definite ideas about the use of colour.

> *Useful language*
>
> Stating purposes:
>   We'll use cherry red paint to give an illusion of warmth.
>   We'll use the same colour throughout to give a sense of unity.
>   We'll put in big mirrors for more light and to make the rooms look bigger.
>   We'll use a simple design to create a calm atmosphere.
>
> Expressing doubt:
>   Will you really be able to make the rooms look bigger?
>   We hardly need mirrors in every room, do we?
>   I dare say you're right about the red paint, but I think I'd prefer white.

6.8 Swap-a-house holidays ☆

You have just joined an association which will enable you to have cheap holidays anywhere in the world by exchanging your accommodation with people who want to come to your country. The association has asked you to write a short description of your own home for their bulletin. You should not only describe the number of rooms, etc., but also indicate the style and atmosphere.

6.9 Discussion

Does it matter if you have taste or if you haven't?
Can taste be acquired or is it inborn?
What is your taste in other areas – music, painting, the opposite sex?
Are there national differences in taste?
Are there historical differences in taste?

7 Brain fever

7.1 What's your brain power?

Try to solve these problems with a partner. Only check your answers (on page 101) after a good try!

1 How many squares do you see?

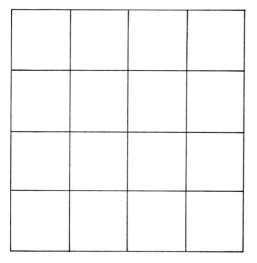

2 Look at the sketch and imagine that you are the person standing in this room. You have been given the task of tying together the ends of two strings suspended from the ceiling. The strings are located so that you cannot reach one string with your outstretched hand while holding the second in your hand. You can imagine that the room contains all the things you might need for solving the problem. Try to find as many different solutions as you can. There is no time limit.

3 (a) When my mother was 41 years old, I was 9. Now she is twice as old as I am. How old am I?

(b) How can you make four 9's equal 100?

(c) Can you make eight 8's equal 1000?

4 (a) You go to bed at 8 o'clock in the evening and set the alarm to get up at 9 in the morning. How many hours of sleep would this allow you?

(b) One month has 28 days. Of the remaining 11 months, how many have 30 days?

(c) Why can't a man living in New York, N.Y., be buried west of the Mississippi?

(d) If you stand on a hard marble floor, how can you drop a raw egg five feet without breaking its shell?

(e) Two fathers and two sons shot three deer. Yet each took home one deer. How was that possible?

(f) How many times can you subtract the numeral 2 from the numeral 24?

(g) A farmer has 4 7/9 haystacks in one corner of the field and 5 2/9 haystacks in another corner of his field. If he puts them all together, how many haystacks will he have?

(h) You won a prize in a contest and could choose either a truckload of nickels or half a truckload of dimes. Which would you choose? (Both trucks are identical in size and shape.)

(i) You are sitting in a room with 12 friends. Can any of them seat themselves in any particular place in this room where it would be impossible for you to do so?

(j) After a woman was blindfolded, a man hung up her hat. She walked 50 feet, turned around, and shot a bullet through her hat. How was she able to do this?

nickel: coin of the U.S. and Canada worth 5 cents
dime: coin of the U.S. and Canada worth 10 cents, smaller in size than a nickel

7.2 Pure logic ☆

By now you should be able to answer this quiz easily! Work with a partner.

1 In a certain African village there live 800 women. Three per cent of them are wearing one earring. Of the other 97 per cent, half are wearing two earrings, half are wearing none. How many earrings altogether are being worn by the women?

2 A logician with some time to kill in a small town decided to have his hair cut. The town only had two barbers, each with his own shop. The logician glanced into one shop and saw that it was extremely untidy. The barber needed a shave, his clothes were unkempt, his hair was badly cut. The other shop was extremely neat. The barber was freshly shaved and spotlessly dressed, his hair neatly trimmed. The logician returned to the first shop for his haircut. Why?

3 A secretary types four letters to four people and addresses the four envelopes. If she inserts the letters at random, each in a different envelope, what is the probability that exactly three letters will go into the right envelopes?

4 If you took three apples from a basket that held 13 apples, how many apples would you have?

5 If nine thousand, nine hundred and nine pounds is written as £9,909, how should twelve thousand, twelve hundred and twelve pounds be written?

6 A chemist discovered that a certain chemical reaction took 80 minutes when he wore a tweed jacket. When he was not wearing the jacket, the same reaction always took an hour and 20 minutes. Explain.

7 A customer in a restaurant found a dead fly in his coffee. He sent the waiter back for a fresh cup. After a sip he shouted, 'This is the *same* cup of coffee I had before!' How did he know?

8 'I guarantee,' said the pet-shop salesman, 'that this parrot will repeat every word it hears.' A customer bought the parrot but found it would not speak a single word. Nevertheless, the salesman told the truth. Can you explain?

You will find the answers on page 102.

Do you know any similar problems of logic? If so, write them down and try them out on a partner.

7.3 A famous puzzler's logic ☆

Lewis Carroll, the author of the famous children's book, *Alice in Wonderland*, earned his living as a lecturer in mathematics at Oxford, and was also extremely interested in puzzles. The ones that follow are taken from his book *Symbolic Logic*.

Draw conclusions from the statements made. Write down the answers. Make sure you have written a proper sentence.

A
1 Babies are illogical;
2 Nobody is despised who can manage a crocodile;
3 Illogical persons are despised.

B
1 My saucepans are the only things I have that are made of tin;
2 I find all *your* presents useful;
3 None of my saucepans is of the slightest use.

C
1 No potatoes of mine, that are new, have been boiled;
2 All my potatoes in this dish are fit to eat;
3 No unboiled potatoes in this dish are fit to eat.

D
1 Everyone who is sane can do logic;
2 No lunatics are fit to serve on a jury;
3 None of *your* sons can do logic.

E
1 No experienced person is incompetent;
2 Jenkins is always blundering;
3 No competent person is always blundering.

F
1 No one takes in *The Times* unless he is well-educated;
2 No hedge-hogs can read;
3 Those who cannot read are not well-educated.

G
1 All puddings are nice;
2 This dish is a pudding;
3 No nice things are wholesome.

H
1 All the old articles in this cupboard are cracked;
2 No jug in this cupboard is new;
3 Nothing in this cupboard, that is cracked, will hold water.

blundering: making clumsy mistakes
wholesome: good for you

You will find the answers on page 102.

7.4 Brain of Britain contest

This is a radio competition which is won by the contestant who can answer correctly more obscure factual questions than the other contestants.

Each student provides one or two general knowledge questions written on a slip of paper. The questions are collected up. The class chooses a question master and a few contestants. This can be done by voting or by picking names out of a hat. The question master picks out the slips of paper at random and asks the contestants questions in turn. A contestant gets two points for every question he or she answers right. If he or she cannot answer the question, the points go to the first of the other contestants to come up with the right answer.

7.5 Role-play: the Brain of Britain

This year's winner is being interviewed by a journalist.

B.R. HAYNE
You have just won the Brain of Britain contest for the third time running. You are being interviewed by a journalist about how you have managed to acquire so much knowledge. You will also be asked for advice for young hopefuls.

LES POWER
You are a journalist who is interviewing B.R. Hayne about his / her repeated successes in the Brain of Britain contest. You are sure that he / she has some special secret that you are determined to elicit. You also ask him / her for advice for young contenders who are entering the contest for the first time.

> *Useful language*
>
> Making recommendations:
>   If I were a youngster nowadays, I'd be much more systematic than I used to be.
>   He / she would have no chance of success unless he / she were prepared to work very hard.
>   If a youngster is looking for success, he / she will find it through persistence and hard work.
>   If I were a youngster preparing for the contest, I'd read a chunk from an encyclopedia every day.

7.6 The brain age ☆

Some people say that brain power declines with age. Others claim that we have more cells in our brains than we could ever use and that it is lack of practice rather than lack of ability that makes our mental performance decrease. Poets have been said to produce their best work between 25 and 30, scientists between 30 and 34, medical men and philosophers between 35 and 39 and fiction writers between 30 and 45. But these figures are just averages. Make a list of all the exceptions you know. Use examples from your private life as well as public figures. Discuss your list with a partner.

7.7 Mind maps ☆

Getting one's brain to work efficiently is often simply a question of good organisation. Look at the way information is organised in this chart.

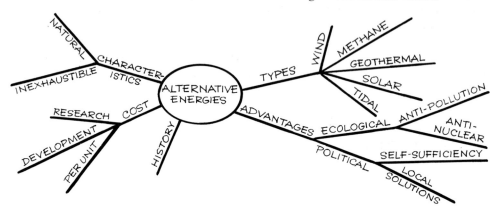

Now make your own mind map on a topic of your choice. Improvise from it a two-minute talk for your class or for a small group in your class. Some suggested topics:
cinema
space exploration
your work
your favourite leisure interest
the history of your country

7.8 Your mental achievements

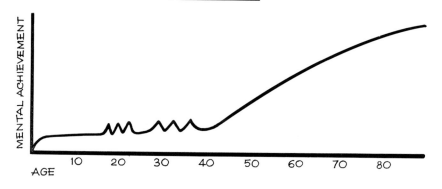

This is the mental achievement graph of a slow learner who had many ups and downs in the early part of his life, but whose mental powers then increased until he died at a ripe old age.

Plot your own peaks of mental achievement on a graph. Discuss the graph with a partner.

7.9 Are you a genius? ☆

There is an international organisation, Mensa, whose only requirement for membership is an I.Q. in the 'genius' range. Try this test and see if you are eligible. Time yourself: there are bonus points for finishing in less than 15, 20 or 25 minutes.

1 Which of the lower boxes best completes the series on the top?

(a)　　　(b)　　　(c)　　　(d)

2 I am a man. If Larry's son is my son's father, what relationship am I to Larry?

(a) His grandfather　　(d) His grandson
(b) His father　　　　(e) I am Larry
(c) His son　　　　　 (f) His uncle

3 Which word does not belong in the following group?

(a) Knife　　(c) Smile　　(e) Lovely
(b) Swan　　(d) Feather　(f) Thought

4 Which two shapes below represent mirror images of the same shape?

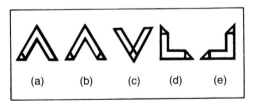
(a)　(b)　(c)　(d)　(e)

5 What number comes next in this series?

9, 16, 25, 36....

6 Complete this analogy with a five-letter word ending with letter 'H'. High is to low as sky is to ----H.

7 In the box below, a rule of arithmetic applies across and down the box so that two of the numbers in a line produce the third. What is the missing number?

```
6  2  4
2  ?  0
4  0  4
```

8 Complete this analogy with a seven-letter word ending with the letter 'T'. Potential is to actual as future is to ------T.

9 In the group below, find the two words whose meanings do not belong with the others.

(a) glue　　　(d) nail
(b) sieve　　 (e) string
(c) buzz saw　(f) paper clip

10 Mountain is to land as whirlpool is to:

(a) forest　　(c) sea　　(e) shower
(b) wet　　　(d) sky

11 Find the number that logically completes the series:

2, 3, 5, 9, 17....

12 Two of the shapes below represent mirror images of the same shape. Which are they?

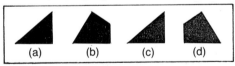
(a)　　(b)　　(c)　　(d)

13 Statistics indicate that men drivers are involved in more accidents than women drivers. The only conclusion that can certainly be drawn is that:

(a) Male chauvinists are wrong, as usual, about women's abilities.
(b) Men are actually better drivers but drive more frequently.
(c) Men and women drive equally well, but men log more total mileage.
(d) Most truck drivers are men.
(e) There is not enough information to justify a conclusion.

14 In the box below, a rule of arithmetic applies across and down the box so that two of the numbers in a line produce the third. What is the missing number?

```
 6   2  12
 4   5  20
24  10   ?
```

15 If A × B = 24, C × D = 32 B × D = 48 and B × C = 24, what does A × B × C × D equal?

(a) 480 (c) 744 (e) 824
(b) 576 (d) 768

16 Which of the four lower selections best completes the series on the top?

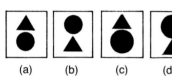

(a) (b) (c) (d)

17 Which word does not belong in this group?

(a) microscope   (d) telescope
(b) magnifying glass (e) telegraph
(c) microphone

18 Find the two words nearest in meaning to each other.

(a) beam   (c) giggle   (e) collection
(b) lump   (d) ray

19 If Jim turns right *or* left at the stop sign he will run out of gas before he reaches a service station. He has already gone too far past a service station to return before he runs out of gas. He does not see a service station ahead. Only one of the following statements can be positively deduced:

(a) He may run out of gas.
(b) He will run out of gas.
(c) He should not have taken this route.
(d) He is lost.
(e) He should turn right at the stop sign.
(f) He should turn left at the stop sign.

20 Complete the following analogy

as + − 0 are to:

(a) + − 0   (c) − + 0   (e) + + 0
(b) 0 + −   (d) 0 − +

You will find the answers on page 102.

How to score

Give yourself one point for each correct answer. You receive an additional five points if you finished the test in less than 15 minutes, three points if you finished in less than 20 minutes, and two points if you finished in less than 25 minutes. If you scored:

20-25 points: You are extremely intelligent – a perfect candidate for Mensa.

15–19 points: This should put you in the higher percentiles of the population – definitely a Mensa candidate.

10–14: Nothing to be ashamed of – a most respectable score. You should probably try the complete, standard Mensa test.

Fewer than 10 points: Forget about joining Mensa, but don't stew about it. You may just be having a bad day. Some of the most successful writers, businessmen, artists and other famous people don't have exceptionally high I.Q.s, either.

7.10 Discussion

The nature versus nurture debate: do we inherit our I.Q. or is it the result of our environment and upbringing?
Have I.Q. and intelligence got anything to do with creativity and genius?
Does I.Q. vary according to sex?
Does being intelligent matter, or are other things more important?
Are puzzles, intelligence tests and so on a waste of time?
What do you know about the left and right brain hemispheres?

8 Beyond reason

8.1 Your superstitious beliefs – a quick check

Do this quiz with a partner.

1. Do you believe it is unlucky to walk under a ladder?
2. When you tell someone about something that you hope is going to happen, do you ever touch wood or cross your fingers, or do you feel a strong urge to do so?
3. Are you the slightest bit bothered by the number 13?
4. Have you got a lucky number?
5. Do you read your horoscope regularly?
6. Have you ever consulted a fortune teller, palmist, etc?
7. Have you ever thrown a coin into a wishing well?
8. Have you ever made a decision after consulting a deck of cards, playing patience, etc?
9. Is there a particular day of the week which is lucky or unlucky for you?
10. Have you ever changed your plans because of a dream?
11. Have you any kind of talisman or lucky object?
12. Do you believe in any other superstitious customs of your own country?

Now check your score on page 103.

Analysis

Less than 4: You are very hard-headed and have virtually no trace of superstitious tendencies or beliefs. This is very unusual. Are you sure you answered the questions honestly?

Between 4 and 12: This is a very low score and suggests you are a very practical person and perhaps in a profession where facts and figures are more important than hunches and inspirations.

Between 12 and 24: People in this bracket usually have a good mixture of scepticism and flexibility in the way they relate to the unexplained areas of experience. For you, the superstitions of today may well be the facts of tomorrow.

8.2 A supernatural survey

With a partner make notes on your beliefs on the following subjects. Then compare notes with the rest of the class.

Do you believe in:	Y/N	If yes, what evidence?	If no, why not?
Ghosts			
Astrology			
Talking to plants to make them grow better			
Dowsing			
Faith healing			
Telepathy			
Mediums			
Other			

dowsing: looking for underground sources of water with a divided twig or a special piece of apparatus

Useful language

coincidence　　cynical
genuine　　　　reincarnation
hoax　　　　　subconscious
fake　　　　　water-divining
fraud
proof

8.3 Telepathy

Try this simple telepathy experiment with a partner.
Sit in two separate rooms or at opposite ends of the same room. Number a sheet from 1 – 10. Look at the symbols below that are commonly used in telepathy experiments. One person fixes his or her mind on one of the symbols for 10 seconds, notes it against number 1 and then moves on to another one. The other person attempts to tune into the thoughts of his or her partner and notes down the symbol. When you have tried it 10 times, check your symbols against your partner's.

N.B. Remember to synchronise your watches.

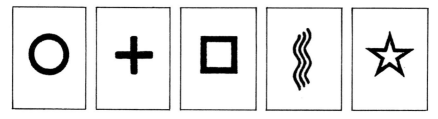

Any score of more than 4 indicates real potential!

8.4 Supernatural conversation

Work in groups of about six people. Within each group divide up into three pairs. Each pair reads one of the following articles. Then, one person begins by recounting the anecdote he or she has read and giving reasons for believing or disbelieving it. The other members of the group give their own reactions. The same procedure is used for the other two anecdotes.

The Nottingham Lion

Two milkmen were the first to report having seen the Nottingham lion in July 1976. They told policemen that it was during their morning round in a village near Nottingham that they saw the animal. Although they had only had a back view, they were convinced of its identity because of its size, its tawny colour and its bushy tail. The milkmen appeared to be reliable and sensible witnesses, and the police began a lion hunt.

During the week that the pursuit lasted, the police received 65 reports of sightings. The lion, however, was appearing in places too far apart for most of the sightings to be taken seriously and it soon became obvious that various household pets or even a wind-blown brown paper bag were being mistaken for the 'lion'. When all the zoos and circuses in the country had been checked and it was obvious that no lion had escaped, the police dropped the hunt.

The Bermuda Triangle

Flight 19 should have been routine. It was a normal training flight from the Naval Air Station at Fort Lauderdale, Fla.—5 TBM Avengers, torpedo bombers equipped with excellent navigational and radio equipment.

One plane had a crew of 2; the others had 3 men each. Their planned course was a triangle — 160 miles east, 40 miles north, then southwest back to the base.

The first sign of trouble came after 1½ hours. By that time, they should have returned to base. Instead, there was a weird radio message from the flight commander, 'Calling tower. This is an emergency . . . We seem to be off course . . . We cannot see land . . . (REPEAT) We cannot see land.'

When asked for their position, he said, 'We are not sure of our position. We can't be sure of just where we are. We seem to be lost.' Then, when told to head due west, he radioed, 'We do not know which way is west. Everything is wrong . . . strange. We can't be sure of any direction. Even the ocean doesn't look as it should.'

At 4:25, the last message came, 'Not certain where we are . . . about 225 miles northeast of base . . . Looks like we are —'

A Martin flying boat with a crew of 13 men took off to begin a search for the missing planes. Five minutes later, it vanished. Six planes were inexplicably lost.

The Loch Ness Monster

Since W.W.II, the monster has been taken very seriously. In October, 1954, the passengers on a bus driving by the lake were able to observe the monster for 10 minutes as it surfaced not more than 100 yards away.

In December, 1954, a fishing boat was crossing the lake when its echo-sounder began to chart something swimming at a depth of 540'. It was recorded as a creature with a small head on a long neck, 8 short legs, and a 15' tail. It measured about 50' in length. Experts who analysed the chart said it was a living thing.

Four years later, the British Broadcasting Company, attempting to produce a program about the monster, recorded an object on the echo-sounder that moved 12' deeper, then disappeared at 60'. Two days after, 4 men riding by on a bus saw humps emerging in the same spot; there was a big wash as the humps submerged.

W.W.II: World War II

You may also discuss other international mysteries (Atlantis, UFO's, etc.) or local mysteries.

Useful language
Talking about certainty and doubt:
  There must be something in it.
  There can't be any truth in such a story.
  It can't have been a real animal.
  Something must have happened to start the rumour off.
  It couldn't have happened like you say it did.
  It may just have been collective hallucination.
  It might really have happened.

8.5 Role-play: the UFO spotter

THE POLICEMAN

A UFO spotter has just phoned the police station. You must fill in the form below provided by a UFO research organisation.

THE SPOTTER

You have just observed a UFO and are phoning in your news to the local police station. You will be asked fairly precise questions, so you must have an accurate picture in mind.

UFO Report Form

1 Place ....
Date ....
Time ....

2 How long was UFO seen for? ....

3 Angle of UFO in the sky (90°, 75°, 60°, 45°, 30°, 15°, 0°)
Position of UFO (N, NE, E, SE, S, SW, W, NW)
Sketch UFO here
(mark on with pencil)

4 Appearance of UFO
Shape ....
Sound ....
Colour ....
Movements...
Number of objects ....
Brightness ....
(Compared to a star, Venus, Moon, Sun, etc.)

5 Name and address of witness (if any) ....
....
....

6 Weather conditions (Tick circle)

Clouds		Temperature		Wind		Precipitation	
Clear sky	○	Cold	○	None	○	Dry	○
Scattered cloud	○	Cool	○	Breeze	○	Fog or mist	○
Much cloud	○	Warm	○	Moderate	○	Rain	○
Overcast	○	Hot	○	Strong	○	Snow	○

Other conditions if any ....

> *Useful language*
>
> Reporting the event: (To gain your listener's attention you will need to use the present perfect tense.)
> > I've just seen an amazing sight.
> > It's the most spectacular UFO that has ever been seen.
> > So far nothing like this has been reported.
>
> (But to report the facts you should use the simple past.)
> > A spot grew bright in the sky.
> > It made very weird sounds.
> > It got nearer and nearer.

8.6 Hitting the headlines ☆

Write a short account of a UFO spotting for the local newspaper. Give details of the UFO itself, the witness and so on. Don't forget the headline.

8.7 The 'night' side of life ☆

Look at this list of types of dreams. Check off each type that you can remember dreaming. Work with a partner. Every time you answer yes, describe the dream in that category to him or her.

		YES	NO
1	Dreams in which you find you can fly or float in the air.	☐	☐
2	Dreams in which you feel very anxious about something.	☐	☐
3	Dreams about the sea.	☐	☐
4	Dreams about the future which came true.	☐	☐
5	Recurring dreams.	☐	☐
6	Dreams about finding money.	☐	☐
7	Dreams in which you discover the 'secret of the universe' or some similar revelation, only to forget it on waking.	☐	☐
8	Dreams about famous people, politicians, film stars, etc.	☐	☐
9	Dreams featuring scenes of violence.	☐	☐
10	Dreams about falling.	☐	☐
11	Dreams in which you are being chased.	☐	☐
12	Dreams in which you are in a strange or unknown house.	☐	☐
13	Dreams in which you are at a party or social gathering.	☐	☐
14	Dreams in which your teeth are breaking or falling out.	☐	☐

Are these dreams common? Are they normal? Read on and find out.

1   Dreams about flying or floating in the air are often considered to be related to an unconscious wish to escape from something. They are in fact reported by about 50% of dreamers.

2   Anxiety dreams are among the most common types reported and are particularly common among women (78%). Only 63% of men experience them.

3   Dreams about the sea, which are reputed to have a sexual interpretation by the Freudians and to represent the unconscious mind by Jungians, are very common indeed. Again, however, women (40%) are far more likely to experience them than men (27%).

4   Dreams about the future which come true are very frequently reported though it is fair to say that scientists are very doubtful about whether these are simply coincidence or genuine peeps into the future. Almost 30% of people believe that they have had at least one such dream.

5   Recurring dreams are very common – 70% of people reporting them on average. In most cases recurring dreams are of a vaguely unpleasant kind and are almost certainly caused because the individual has a problem of a significant kind which he is unable to resolve in his waking life. The solving of his problem almost always leads to the disappearance of the recurring dream. Women are more likely to have recurring dreams than men.

6   This is a relatively common dream, often experienced by people when their finances are tight. Typically it involves finding coins showering from a slot machine or picking them up in great profusion from the ground. About a quarter of men have had this dream, but only 15% of women. This presumably relates to the fact that money matters are more likely to preoccupy the male than the female.

7   Dreams of this kind, which may be either pleasant or unpleasant, are often associated with recovery from a general anaesthetic after having a tooth out or an operation. Such dreams, which are very hard to explain, are in fact surprisingly common with about 17% of people having had them.

8. Women are more likely to dream about famous people, politicians, pop stars and the like (33%) than men (27%). One very common dream, which almost certainly falls into the wish fulfillment category, is when people report that they are actually meeting famous people in their dreams.

9 Dreams featuring scenes of violence are, perhaps predictably, much more common among men (50%) than among women (44%). However the differences are not very great. Perhaps men are simply more likely to talk about violent things and it must be remembered that women are often the most ardent fans of TV Westerns and wrestling programmes.

10 Dreams about falling are very common with about a 75% scoring on average. The most frequently reported is one in which typically, one 'trips over something,' stumbles or falls and wakes up with a jump. Psychologists now believe that these dreams do not necessarily have any great emotional significance but are merely due to muscular spasms which take place on the threshold between consciousness and sleep.

11 Over 70% of people have dreamed that they were being chased or pursued by something, and often in the dream they find themselves unable to flee for one reason or another. These often occur during periods of great anxiety and may be related to frustrating situations which are frequently occurring in their waking life.

12 A very curious and common dream (31%) is one in which the sleeper finds himself wandering in a strange house full of empty rooms. The psychoanalytic interpretation that this is a disguised sexual dream is not generally accepted today and the present feeling is that this is another class of anxiety dream which reflects a general uneasiness in waking life. Often in such dreams one is looking for something which one never finds and is conscious of a pervading sense of worry.

13 About 31% of people have this dream, and it may take principally two forms. In one, the dreamer is happy and enjoying himself in the group. In the other he is ill at ease. Such dreams tend to relate to such personality variables as extroversion and introversion.

14 This bizarre dream, which may take a number of different forms, may also have a number of different explanations. In psychoanalysis the loss of the teeth is presumed to denote a loss of sexual potency or a fear of such loss. Some psychologists however believe that it is a memory dream referring back to that significant period in your baby life when teeth fell out. A third explanation is that you are suffering from low level toothache which is not enough to get through to the conscious mind but which trickles through into your dreams.

Who dreams about what in your class? Do a class survey and see if it reflects the percentages given in the questionnaire. If your class is mixed, are the male/female percentages respected? What do you think about the sex differences given in these descriptions?

8.8 Discussion

What are the sources of superstition?
What do you know about superstition throughout history?
Does progress mean that superstition will disappear?
Are women more superstitious than men?
How subjective is spatial, visual and auditory perception?
How does the subconscious influence perception?
Are some societies more geared to the subconscious and supernatural than others?
What do you know about hallucination?
What do you know about hypnosis?

9 Your pen personality

9.1 You and your handwriting ☆

To find out what your handwriting gives away, take a sample and check it for the characteristics outlined below. For a more reliable picture, use three or more samples written several months apart. These should be written in ink and on unlined paper. The address of an envelope should not be used as the effort the writer usually makes to be extremely legible causes the writing to be unnatural. The writing should be fairly recent, as changes in handwriting are brought about by the maturing of a personality, and should not be written specially for the test.

Work with a partner, and practise making suggestions about what each other's handwriting reveals.

> *Useful language*
>
> Don't you think...?
> Could it possibly mean that...?
> Perhaps it shows signs of...
> I don't want to upset you, but it looks as if...

Size

The size of a person's handwriting symbolises the person's assessment of him or herself. The average or 'normal' size of a small letter is 3mm. Larger letters may indicate such positive characteristics as seriousness, pride in one's work and generosity, or they may indicate negative characteristics such as arrogance, conceit and boastfulness. The positive aspects of a small script are devotion, humility and tolerance. Alternatively it can mean shyness, lack of self-confidence, fear or faint-heartedness.

In fact I didn't exist.

Love been done before we the Devil looked after his own!!

⇶→

Slant
Writing that slants to the right shows an extroverted and outward going personality which, in its positive aspects, is active, friendly and sympathetic but might also be restless, hasty or even hysterical. An upright script indicates a self-sufficient and reserved nature; the head rules the heart, occasionally to such an extent that the writer may be accused of rigidity and coldness. A left-sloping script with an angle of less than 85 degrees can be interpreted to mean self-control. When the slope is less than 60 degrees, it can mean shyness, withdrawal or fear of the future.

Many thanks for your letter
What a splendid start to the

Width and narrowness
In normal writing the distance between the downstrokes of small letters is equal to the height. Wide writing indicates a warm and vivacious person, whereas narrow writing shows timidity and perhaps inhibition in personal relationships.

to catch my London connection

Connectedness
When four or more letters are written with one stroke the writing is considered to be connected. Breaks for dotting 'i's and crossing 't's do not count. It generally means a co-operative nature, but can mean over-adaptability and a tendency to follow the crowd.

The whole lot

In disconnected script, less than four letters are written with one stroke of the pen. It tends to mean an intuitive, self-reliant and individualistic personality. The negative aspects of such characteristics are egocentricity, inconsistency or loneliness.

disgrace! We have just had

Regularity and irregularity

Regularity, both of size and slant, can be interpreted as resistance and moderation, but may simply be a sign of dullness, coldness and indifference.

keep going. A bit of a problem as I'm rather ignorant about gardening —

The positive aspects of irregularity are impulsiveness, warmth and creativity. Its negative aspects are moodiness, irritability and capriciousness.

David is grown up + both beautiful + virtuous, as well as funny + nice

Direction of lines

Does your writing slope upwards? This may mean you are an ambitious and optimistic person, or alternatively that you often lose your temper or are rather frivolous. If your writing slopes downwards over the page it indicates a pessimistic and over-sensitive nature. But take heart! The direction of the lines is one of the least permanent aspects of our writing and probably only reveals a passing mood.

Loops

Full round loops in the upper zone of the writing ('f's, 'l's, etc.) mean vision, imagination and colourful speech. An absence of loops indicates an analytical mind and strong moral tendencies. Loops in the lower zone tend to indicate erotic fantasies and behaviour, sensuousness, materialism and country interests. Small loops – or no loops at all – show a business mind and realism, but sometimes also pessimism and an obsession with money.

unmistakable array of goods

This sums up pretty well my feelings about a wet weekend

Signatures

Signatures are significant in as much as they differ in size from the rest of the text. A much larger signature shows a person who has an over-blown opinion of him or herself. A much smaller signature indicates a shy and retiring personality. Differences of size, angle and width between the christian name and the family name symbolise the relationship between the writer and his or her family.

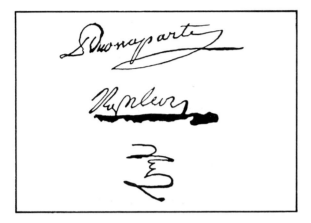

The rise and fall of Napoleon. Top to bottom, signatures of Captain Buonaparte, Emperor of the French, and exile of St Helena.

9.2 Personality traits ☆

In this section you can check someone's handwriting for specific characteristics. Do not draw any too definite conclusions, however. A professional graphologist would never dream of doing a partial analysis like this!

Adventurousness: large upper and lower zones but a normal size middle zone, originality, lack of ornamentation and good spacing
Aggressiveness: angles, speed, heavy pressure
Amiability: connectedness, low 't' bars, a right slope
An analytical mind: a sharp script, simplified and with good spacing
Broad-mindedness: small writing, an upright script
Courage: heavy pressure, particularly on the final strokes, a good distribution of space
Directness: omission of initial strokes and simplification
Dishonesty: the bottoms of rounded letters (a, o, d, etc.) are not closed
Far-sightedness: large regular script
Humour: wavy, horizontal strokes
Intuition: disconnected script
Moodiness: irregular script
Optimism: ascending lines and 't' bars, high-placed 'i' dots, firm strokes, wide and slanting script
Thoughtfulness: upright writing, careful placing of 'i' dots and 't' bars, sharpness and regularity
Tolerance: small upright script with short 't' bars

9.3 Thumbnail portraits ☆

We often judge people by their handwriting. It has been reported that many teachers systematically give better marks to students whose writing is neat and legible. When our friends write to us we judge their writing in the same way as we judge the way they dress. But should we be doing so? Thumbnail sketches, which were devised by two psychologists, Allport and Vernon, give a fairly accurate idea of the dominant features of personality.

Can you match the following samples with the descriptions? Give the reasons for your choice before looking at the answers, which you will find on page 103.

A highly artistic, hyper-active, generous and cheerful bohemian

B colourless, quiet, agreeable and dependable student

C immature, self-assertive, extravagant, unstable student

D forceful, active, efficient businessman, but cautious and exact

9.4 Feminine writing and masculine writing ☆

A number of studies on handwriting have shown that even somebody with no training in graphology whatever has more than chance success in detecting the sex of the writer. Try your own ability with these three samples:

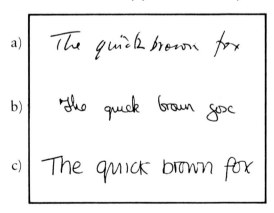

You will find the answers on page 103.

If you are in a mixed class, collect samples from the class and see if you can determine the sex of the writer.

9.5 Professional advice

Look at the graphologer's analysis of this letter.

> Jaspers Cottage
> Patmore Heath
> Albury
> Ware
> Hertfordshire
>
> Dear Gill and André,
>
> I'm sitting here by the log fire, all very cosy, while it's bitterly cold outside with traces of snow still lingering on the ground. To cheer me up I've just written two letters to France - one to Camping l'Airial and one to Camping La Paillotte, both in the Landes close to Hossegor by Lac du Soustons. We hope to be camping there this summer between 20 July and 5 August and hope very much that we can see you whilst we are there.
>
> That also prompts me to answer the question raised in your letter to us recently! We would be pleased to welcome the French girl into our humble abode (does she have an older sister?) but perhaps you could tell us when she would like to come, for how long, and what her parents would think of as a reasonable rent. As you can see from the above dates, she would have to come either in early July or from the middle of August.

A professional graphologer says:

The writer gives a first impression of being a composed and well-balanced personality. However he is in fact fairly emotional and sensitive. He has a far more passionate nature than his undemonstrative exterior would seem to indicate. He is meticulous and consistent in everything he does and in his work he is precise and methodical. He has a logical and rigorous mind and is able to concentrate for long periods at a time. His imagination and intuition are not highly developed and he is slow to take initiative. His contribution to society lies in his circumspect and careful judgements. He is very conscientious and takes life rather seriously.

Collect samples of handwriting from the class. The samples should be distributed at random and an analysis of each sample written for homework. Then compare your impressions with the reality!

9.6 Doodling

Our personality can apparently be revealed not only by what we write but also by what we draw. Copy the following shapes onto a blank sheet of paper. Draw as spontaneously as possible on the front face only of each cube.

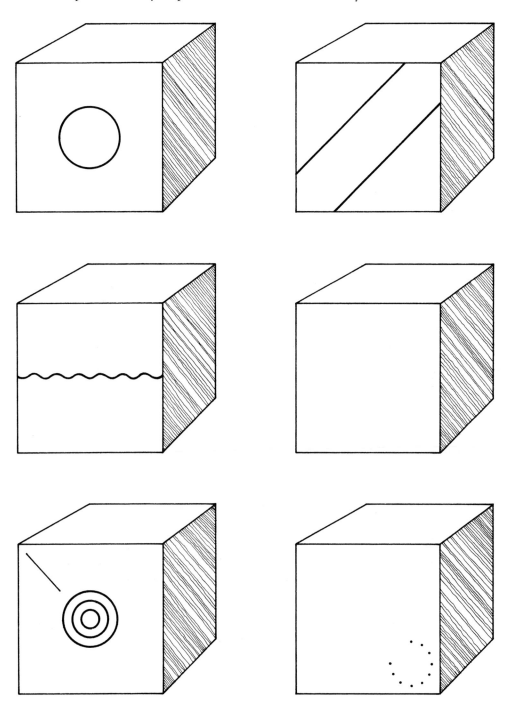

Analysis

1 Self-image

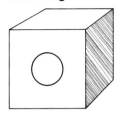

In this square you have drawn the image you have of yourself. If you have sketched a funny face, you are good-natured, tactful and have a sense of humour. A ridiculous or ugly face reflects the difficulty you have in developing personal relationships. A sun indicates a strong and dominating personality with a great deal of self-confidence. A flower is a symbol of femininity – you like to be surrounded by friends and are proud of your physical appearance. If you have drawn a regular pattern, you are one of those people who are always wondering if they have turned the tap off or if they have remembered to lock the front door; you are also very demanding. An eye reveals that you are proud and suspicious and that you attempt to control your life and your relationships with other people. If you have drawn anything else, you should interpret it yourself (you may, for instance, have represented yourself as a bomb or a balloon!) and your friends might help you by telling you how they see you.

2 Friendship

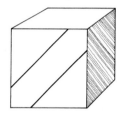

In this square most people draw several separate shapes which are quite distinct. The more shapes there are, the more friends you have. Any drawing inside the parallel lines indicates that you have strong friendships in one or more distinct social groups (family, social milieu, office, school). Drawing outside the parallel lines shows that you only have intermittent relationships or friendships with people. If these shapes are linked together, you have a nostalgia for more durable relationships. One simple line between the two bars suggests that you are reserved, and egocentric. If you sketch a box (or a coffin) you are a solitary person and have a tendency to be moody. Women who draw perpendicular parallel lines have mostly male friendships and are more romantic. Men who draw circular patterns seek the company of women. Short lines or Xs inside the lines indicate that you only appreciate close and lasting relationships. Such people have no time for superficial friendships.

3 Self-confidence

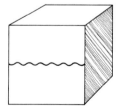

If you have drawn above the line, you feel at ease in your environment. Many people draw a boat. If this boat is rocking, you feel very secure. If you have drawn under the line, you lack self-confidence and feel insecure. If you have drawn both above and below the line, decide which part is more significant. If you have drawn someone drowning, you are afraid of the future. If you have made some kind of pattern or chain which is not linked to the line, you are hard-working, conscientious and seldom make an error.

4 Major interest

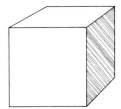

In this square what you have drawn represents your major interest in life, what is most important to you, something fairly secret perhaps. You will probably have to interpret it yourself. However, if you have drawn someone of your own sex, you are yourself the centre of interest in your life. (Why not?) A landscape or a still life indicate artistic gifts. If you have drawn nothing in this square, you should open your eyes and see that there actually are interesting people and things about.

5 Aspirations

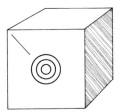

An arrow pointing directly towards the target indicates an ambitious nature, and an ability to work towards a set aim. If you have drawn other lines and arrows pointing towards the target, you are ambitious but you also know how to choose. If you avoid the symbol of the arrow and the target and draw something completely different (a bird, a cart, a lollypop), you are independent and a bit of a rebel. You are sure to have passed your exams easily and you belong to that category of people who thinks that the world belongs to those who reach out to grasp it.

6 Imagination

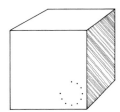

A lot of people are perplexed by the dotted circle in this square. If you integrate the dots into your drawing (through for example, birdseed, a rabbit's tail or ants), you have a vivid imagination. If you turn the dots into a continuous, circular line, you are a pragmatic and logical person with a great deal of practical sense. If you have drawn several circles around the dots, you fear things that escape your control. If you have drawn nothing here, you have no imagination.

General notes
Recurrent faces indicate a sociable nature. Some people do this test hurriedly without getting involved personally. These are reserved and shy people who hide their anxiety beneath an attitude of bravura. They are usually kind, but also a little awkward. People who write on the drawings or give them titles tend to be intellectuals who like abstract ideas. They also like to draw attention to themselves. Drawings which go over the edge of the boxes indicate an unruly nature. Small and detailed drawing indicates a love of perfection and perseverance. Drawings showing perspective indicate an ability to plan ahead. People who put in relief usually succeed in their careers. A horizon line in the box often indicates people who think before they act. People who draw food have the impression that they are not appreciated by other people (food may of course also mean hunger). Shadows in any drawing indicate a sensual nature. Eyes, ears and noses denote suspicion, and clothes, spectacles, or jewels show people who are preoccupied by their physical appearance.

9.7 Letter writing ☆

Write a letter of application for a job in answer to one of the following advertisements.

If you are doing this in preparation for the role-play (9.8), an equal number of students should prepare each advertisement.

PUBLIC RELATIONS OFFICER

The HOUSE BUILDERS FEDERATION, which represents the interests of the private housebuilding industry, is seeking an active creative and highly motivated person aged 25-35 with a knowledge of public affairs to take up the post of Public Relations Officer. Experience of the industry and the housing market would be a distinct advantage but in any case the successful applicant must be prepared to acquire a detailed grasp of the industry and the contribution to its affairs made by HBF.

The Public Relations Officer will be required to write speeches, articles, Press Notices including contributions to the Housebuilder magazine, to organise Press Conferences and briefings, to maintain close personal contact with the media and develop further initiatives as appropriate.

The successful applicant is likely to have a background in either journalism or public relations or specific experience of the private house building industry in terms of promotional or marketing activities which could be adapted and developed to meet the demands of this position.

Applications, marked Private and Confidential, to **Director of Information Services, National Federation of Building Trades Employers, 82 New Cavendish Street, London W1M 8AD,** by 21st April, 1981.

Affiliated to the National Federation of Building Trades Employers

---

THE MIDDLESEX HOSPITAL MEDICAL SCHOOL W.1.

SECRETARY

The Secretary of the Medical School requires a Secretary with previous secretarial experience at senior level involving the exercise of responsibility and initiative.

A knowledge of University procedures would be an advantage, but is not essential. 4 weeks' annual holiday.

Salary on the scale £5,097 – £5,973 per annum acording to age and experience.

Please telephone:
01-638 8333, Ext. 7108.

TRAINEE MAKE-UP ASSISTANTS
£3,750 – £4,595 p.a.
West London

Minimum age 20½. Pleasant personality, tact, and sympathetic manner essential, together with a practical interest in Make-up for Television, Theatre or Film and/or formal training in hairdressing or art. Normal colour vision essential. A good educational standard desirable, preferably with A or O levels in English, Art, and History. Training period two years. Salary enhanced by 15% irregular hours working allowance. The next course is scheduled to start on June 15, 1981. (Ref 2153 GU)

Salaries currently under review.

Relocation expenses considered.

Contact us immediately for application form (quote ref and enclose s.a.e.) **BBC Appointments, London W1A 1AA.** Tel. 01-580 4468, ext. 4619.

Creative Engineer

Electronics/ electromechanical late 20s–early 30s to £18,000 + benefits

Part of a very well-known manufacturing group based in the Home Counties, our client has achieved independent success by continually launching products a quantum leap ahead of the competition's technology. The company now needs an engineer and manager to lead a small team of talented, realistic young engineers in this innovative work. The practical creation of viable new products–with, without or even in spite of a marketing brief–is the crux of this job.

You should be in your late 20s-early 30s, a graduate (preferably in electronics, although this is not a pure electronics role), with experience of electronic controls, mechanisms, etc, for example in consumer durables. Experience of specifying and coordinating injection moulding and sheet metal components from external suppliers is also available. Above all, the need is for someone who can respond to a clear commercial objective by challenging, questioning and inventing rather than by providing the 'obvious' solution. You will see your ideas in production quickly, and your prospects rapidly widen as you get results.

Ring 01-235 3627 (24-hour answering service) to request an application form, or reply to PA Advertising in accordance with the instructions below, quoting ref: 3/S3907/ST.

9.8 Role-play: a new member of staff

A personnel officer, the director of the department or company concerned, his or her assistant and a graphologist decide, from the letters of application from 9.7, who is likely to be the most suitable candidate for a particular job.

> *Useful language*
>
> Giving reasons and explanations:
>   I have doubts about this candidate on account of the emotional instability his / her handwriting indicates.
>   We should accept this candidate because of the drive and energy his / her handwriting shows.
>   Owing to his / her lack of imagination, this candidate is not suitable for this particular job.
>
> Being emphatic:
>   I utterly disagree with you.
>   You have scarcely / hardly considered the Smith file.
>   I deeply regret the lack of discussion on this candidate.
>   I thoroughly / absolutely / entirely agree with you.
>   You would clearly / obviously like to see Smith get the job.

9.9 Discussion

Are personality tests reliable? Do they assess what they are supposed to assess?
Is there a stable aspect to personality structure or does personality change? Has your own personality changed?
When can personality tests be useful and when are they dangerous?
Why assess personality at all?
What is the success of this kind of test? Is it just that we like to hear about ourselves?
Is writing a lost art in the audio-visual age?

10 Our families, our friends

10.1 People in our lives

Study this chart from *Mad*, an American humorous magazine.

AGE	SEX	PEOPLE WHO AFFECT OUR LIVES (IN ORDER OF IMPORTANCE!)
0 to 2 years old	Females	Mother, Pediatrician, Father
	Males	Mother, Pediatrician, Father
3 to 4 years old	Females	Mother, Sitter, Pediatrician, Father
	Males	Mother, Sitter, Pediatrician, Puppy, Father
5 to 8 years old	Females	Friend Next Door, Teacher, Sitter, Kitten, Mother, Father, Grandparents, Relatives
	Males	Friend Next Door, Frog, Favorite Cowboy Star, Cowboy Star's Horse, Dog, Sitter, Mother, Father, Grandparents, Relatives, Teacher
9 to 11 years old	Females	Best Friend, Worst Rival, Teacher, 2nd Best Friend, Boys, Cat, Father, Mother, Sitter, Grandparents, Relatives
	Males	Best Friend, Neighborhood Bully, Little League Coach, 2nd Best Friend, Dog, Mother, Father, Grandparents & Relatives, Teacher, Girls
12 to 14 years old	Females	Best Friend, Boys, Favorite Pop Singer, Father, 2nd Best Friend, 3rd Best Friend, First Male Teacher, Other Teachers, Mother, Grandparents & Relatives, Cat
	Males	Best Friend, Rest of Gang, Favorite Baseball Star, Girls, Mother, Father, Dog, Grandparents & Relatives, Teachers

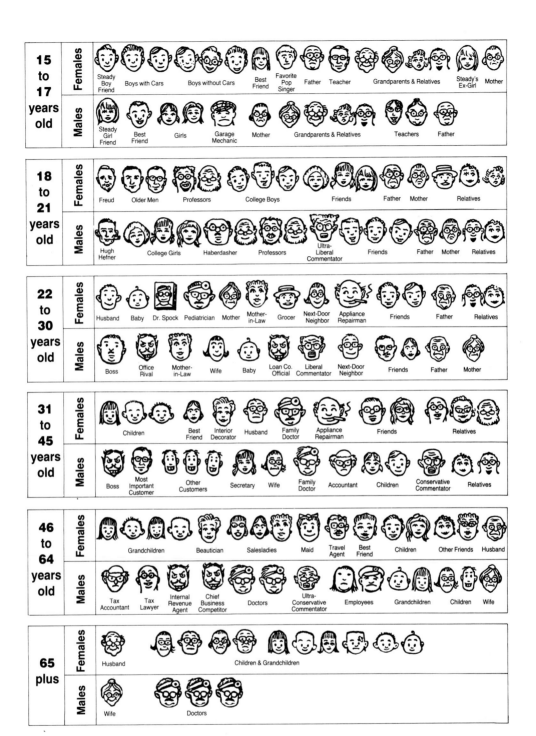

little league coach: coach for boys' baseball team
Hugh Hefner: founder of *Playboy* magazine
haberdasher: (Am.) person selling men's clothes
Dr Spock: famous author of a book on baby care

Who are, or will be, your own 'life-people'? Fill in the chart for yourself. Work with a partner.

| 0 to 2 years old | Females | |
| | Males | |

| 3 to 4 years old | Females | |
| | Males | |

| 5 to 8 years old | Females | |
| | Males | |

| 9 to 11 years old | Females | |
| | Males | |

| 12 to 14 years old | Females | |
| | Males | |

| 15 to 17 years old | Females | |
| | Males | |

| 18 to 21 years old | Females | |
| | Males | |

| 22 to 30 years old | Females | |
| | Males | |

| 31 to 45 years old | Females | |
| | Males | |

| 46 to 64 years old | Females | |
| | Males | |

| 65 plus | Females | |
| | Males | |

Swap life-charts with somebody else. Interview each other about the people on the chart.

10.2 This is your life ☆

a) Write a biography of your partner using the life-chart as a basis.
b) Write an autobiography.

10.3 Your childhood ☆

Do this quiz. Work with a partner.

1. Which of these conditions is closest to those that prevailed in your home?
   a) More or less total confusion with everyone doing more or less what they wanted, making as much noise as they liked.
   b) A certain amount of noise and confusion, but periods of quiet and discipline at certain regular times, for example mealtimes.
   c) Periods of order which slid into confusion until brought together by a burst of parental discipline.
   d) A quiet disciplined house. Everybody let off steam elsewhere.

2. Which of the following is closest to the situation in your house as far as watching the television was concerned?
   a) The TV set was on the whole time whether people were watching it or not.
   b) TV viewing was confined to a few programmes each day and those programmes were specifically selected.
   c) There was no TV in the house.

3. In your family did you:
   a) Have leisure activities that you shared as a family?
   b) Each have your own leisure activity that you pursued individually?
   c) Have no particular leisure activities?

4. As a child did you:
   a) Get regular pocket money?
   b) Earn money for doing jobs around the house?
   c) Get money from your parents according to your needs and whenever you asked for it?
   d) Have no pocket money at all?

5. Did you go to bed:
   a) At a regular bedtime?
   b) At a regular bedtime with exceptions for special occasions?
   c) Whenever you liked?

6. What were the eating habits in your family?
   a) Mealtimes were regular and social occasions.
   b) Mealtimes were chaotic and rushed.
   c) Everybody ate when and where they liked, helping

themselves out of the refrigerator.

7 Who did the housework, shopping, cooking, etc?
a) Your mother.
b) Your mother and father more or less equally.
c) The whole family participated.
d) A maid did everything.

8 If you behaved badly, were you:
a) Reprimanded severely?
b) Given any kind of corporal punishment?
c) Punished in any other way?
d) Not reprimanded at all?

9 With your parents, did you:
a) Talk about any subject under the sun?
b) Talk about most things, except one or two taboo subjects such as sex?
c) Not communicate freely on most subjects?

10 In your home, were other people, family and friends:
a) Always welcome?
b) Sometimes welcome?
c) Never welcome?

Now check your score on page 103.

Analysis

35–50: Your family life was easy-going and free of constraints. This is in line with the modern theory of upbringing, in which self-fulfilment is considered more important than restraint. However, over-indulgent or over-lenient parents are sometimes just the kind of people who cannot cope with family life or who are too busy elsewhere to be very much concerned with what goes on at home.

20–35: This score reflects a balanced and reasonable family life. You were probably not allowed to get away with just anything as a child, but had understanding and caring parents who put a great deal of thought into creating a happy home environment.

less than 20: This score suggests a fairly severe and austere family background. However, it may just be a sign of a more traditional upbringing, for fashions in child-rearing have changed considerably over the last 20 or 30 years.

10.4 Family relationships

Divide the class up into four groups, according to their position in the family: eldest, youngest, middle or only child. Each group discusses what it was like having that particular role in the family. Try to remember precise events which reflect parental attitudes, relationships with brothers and sisters, etc.

10.5 Are you a good judge of character? ☆

Do this quiz to find out.

Study the following twelve pictures carefully. Answer the questions for every picture by ticking what in your view is the correct answer (a, b, or c).

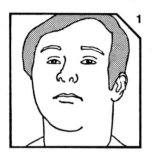

1 Which one of the following characteristics would you most readily connect with this face?

  a meekness
  b contempt
  c insecurity

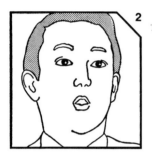

2 Which one of the following characteristics would you most readily connect with this face?

  a rapture
  b anxiety
  c surprise

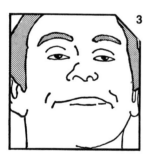

3 Which one of the following characteristics would you most readily connect with this face?

  a disdain
  b anger
  c joy

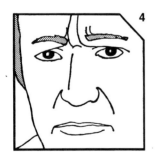

4 Which one of the following characteristics would you most readily connect with this face?

  a grief
  b anger
  c distaste

5 Which one of the following characteristics would you most readily connect with this face?

   a irritation
   b anxiety
   c mistrust

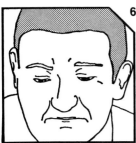

6 Which one of the following characteristics would you most readily connect with this face?

   a fear
   b sentimentality
   c concentration

7 Which one of the following qualities would you most readily connect with this person?

   a matter-of-factness
   b sociability
   c toughness

8 Which one of the following qualities would you most readily connect with this person?

   a matter-of-factness
   b sociability
   c toughness

9 Which person is more intelligent?

   a person 1
   b person 2
   c don't know

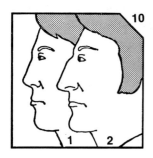

10 Which face conveys greater boldness?

a face 1
b face 2
c don't know

Flowing pleasant sounding voice

11 Which one of these qualities would you associate with a person who speaks like this?

a shyness
b sadness
c serenity

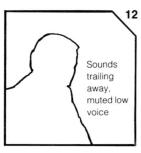

Sounds trailing away, muted low voice

12 Which one of these qualities would you associate with a person who speaks like this?

a embarrassment
b distaste
c reserve

You will find the answers on page 103.

Your test result analysed

Check how good a judge of character you are on the chart:

Points	Judgement of character
10–12	very strong
8–9	strong
6–7	average to strong
4–5	average to weak
0–3	weak

Very strong You are an excellent judge of character. You succeed almost invariably in drawing correct conclusions from the behaviour and external appearance (facial expression, physique, voice) of other people. You are not easily deceived by others.

Strong You are a good judge of character. Most of the time you manage correctly to assess and judge other people.

Average to strong Your skill as a judge of character is within the normal range, tending to be rather more strongly developed.

Average to weak Your skill as a judge of character is within the normal range, but you do not always manage spontaneously to assess others correctly. Try to pay more attention to the study of other people's facial expressions and gestures as a guide to the interpretation of their character.

Weak The evaluation of others from their outward appearance is not your strong point. Unless you are prepared to risk your weakness being exploited, you would be well advised to try to become a better judge of character by more careful observation and by improving your sensitivity.

10.6 What is a friend?

Is a friend someone to talk to? Someone to play tennis with? Someone to rely on?

Make a list of the most important qualities of your friends. Work with a partner.

> *Useful language*
> Talking about people:
>   Someone to share your leisure interests with.
>   Someone to spend your holidays with.
>   Someone you can count on.
>   Someone interesting.

10.7 Role-play: famous friends

ALEX PATTERSON

You have a friend who has just become very famous – decide who he or she is; a sportsman, musician or writer, for example. You are being interviewed by a journalist about your friend whom you admire greatly.

JOURNALIST

You are interviewing Alex Patterson about a friend of his or hers who has just become very famous. Before you start, agree upon the basic profile of the friend.

> *Useful language*
> Talking about people:
>   He / she is much admired for his / her professionalism.
>   He / she is keenly interested in everything his / her friends do.
>   His / her generosity is widely-known.
>   He / she is a very good-natured person.
>   He / she is always well-intentioned, even when he / she makes a blunder.

10.8 Somebody special ☆

Most people have somebody special in their lives. How well do you know that person in your life? Do this quiz, with that special person if you can. Then correct each other's work:

1 What book has your spouse* read most recently?
2 Can you list every pet your spouse has owned, including childhood family pets?
3 For whom did your spouse vote in the last general election?
4 What is your spouse's shoe size?
5 Did your spouse collect anything as a child? What?
6 What's your spouse's favourite fruit?
7 Who is your spouse's best friend?
8 What household chore does your spouse hate most?
9 Does your spouse remember where you went on your first date together?
10 Does your spouse weigh him/herself at least once a week?
11 What was your spouse's first job? (Include part-time jobs as a youngster.)
12 Who's your spouse's favourite relative, outside the immediate family?
13 Who's the *least* favourite?
14 What's your spouse's shirt/dress size?
15 If your spouse could choose any car in the world, which would it be? (A bonus point if you know the colour.)
16 How often does your spouse wash his/her hair?
17 If your spouse was limited to one television programme a week, what's the one he/she couldn't do without?
18 What's your spouse's favourite restaurant?
19 What item of clothing did your spouse most recently buy for him/herself?
20 Can your spouse recite his/her car registration number?

*'Spouse' according to the dictionary means husband or wife. It has been left in this quiz to avoid the complicated terminology that refers to 'life companions' or 'girl / boyfriends' in modern British and American society.

Scoring

Above 18: Very impressive.
14–17: Not bad, but pay more attention.
Below 14: Better consider a crash course; you're not paying attention.

10.9 Togetherness ☆

What are the things you do or would like to do with or without your 'spouse'?
Make a list. Compare your list with someone else's and discuss your choices.

10.10 Discussion

What is the state of the family in the twentieth century?
Why is the divorce rate rising so fast in the western world?
How has the liberation of women affected the family?
Do children make or break a marriage?
What is a friend?
Do men make better friends than women or vice versa?
Can one be 'just friends' with the opposite sex?
What is it like to live alone, outside the structure of a family?
What other social structures do you know about (communes, kibbutzes, etc.)?

11 Left, right and centre

11.1 What's your opinion? ☆

This quiz is designed to test your social attitudes. Work through it with a partner. For each statement mark + + if you strongly agree, + if you tend to agree, ○ if you have no particular opinion, − if you tend to disagree and − − if you strongly disagree.

1. People should not be able to obtain a better education or better medical care for their families by paying for them.
2. Blood sports, like fox-hunting, should be made illegal.
3. Homosexuality should never be treated as a crime.
4. All young men and women should undergo a period of military training, even in peacetime.
5. Capital punishment is a deterrent to would-be murderers.
6. Soft drugs like marijuana should be made legal.
7. People who live in a welfare state tend to lose all sense of initiative.
8. There is nothing wrong with people living together before they are married.
9. In certain circumstances, censorship of the press, literature, films, etc. is justifiable.
10. Trade unions are a hindrance to industrial progress.
11. A person should be entitled to take his or her own life without society interfering, if he or she wishes to do so.
12. Royalty and nobility are incompatible with democracy.
13. It is unfair that some people inherit vast incomes while other people have to work for a living.
14. Most strikes are the result of bad management.
15. It is normal that the police should tap telephones when investigating a crime.
16. Young people with beards and long hair are unpleasant to look at.
17. Human nature being what it is, war is unavoidable.
18. There is nothing wrong with fare-dodging on a bus or train if you can get away with it.

19 All kinds of discrimination against coloured races, Jews, etc., should be illegal and severely punished. ....

20 Men are not created equal. Therefore social inequality is inevitable. ....

---

fare-dodging: avoiding the payment of the fare

Check your score on page 104.

Analysis

85–100: You are on the extreme liberal end of the social scale. Your strong ideals probably make you an active supporter of human rights movements and lead you to defend the underdog. However your view of society may lean a little too far towards the permissive and libertarian to be practicable.

40–85: Your ideals are still showing, but your feet are firmly on the ground. You have a realistic attitude to the actual workings of the social machine without wanting to interfere too much with individual freedom. You maintain the balance between the radical and conservative tendencies that are present in all of us.

Less than 40: You are likely to be extremely right-wing and have a strong authoritarian streak. You are a great believer in law and order, something of a traditionalist and not prepared to change your attitudes very easily.

N.B. This analysis is valid for British society in the 1980s. Your own score may reflect the more liberal or more conservative society in which you live, and should be adjusted accordingly.

11.2 Social reform

Make a list of the ten most urgent measures for social reform in your own country. If you are working in a group, do this in three stages.

a) Have a brain-storming session in which all ideas are noted down by the group leader. The wilder the ideas the better, and no criticism is allowed.
b) The group decides on the ten measures to be retained and the order in which they should be classified. The other suggestions are eliminated.
c) Compare your list with other groups.

Useful language

housing
council houses
private property
salaries

wages
creches
kindergartens
community centres

Precise propositions:
 childcare
 healthcare
 slum improvement
 minority rights

divorce procedure
birth control
prison reform
government interference

11.3 Speaker's Corner

As you walk past Hyde Park in London you may see people speaking out on subjects that are dear to them. They are allowed to say what they like about whom they like. Freedom of speech is sacred. People sometimes talk about important political issues, such as unilateral disarmament or the preservation of the environment, and sometimes about more minor matters such as licensing hours in pubs, the price of a dog licence, the legalisation of soft drugs, etc.

In groups of six or seven, make your own Speaker's Corner. Form a semi-circle. Place a vacant chair in front of the group. Any member of the group is allowed to get up and sit in the empty chair and speak on the subject of his or her choice. A time limit may be set.

11.4 A debate

Debating is a popular activity in British schools and universities. It is a formal exchange of views on a subject, and an attempt on the part of the speaker to convert other people to his or her own point of view. A debate is carried out in the following way:

A motion is set, for example: 'This house believes that censorship in the arts can never be justified'.
Two people volunteer to propose the motion, and two people to oppose the motion.
The speakers each prepare a two-minute speech. They speak alternately, beginning with the proposer. The other speakers may of course have to modify what they say according to what the previous speakers have said.
'The house', or the public, is allowed to ask questions and finally a vote is taken to see who has argued more convincingly.

Carry out a debate on one of the following subjects:
The freedom of the press should be absolute.
Easy divorce is a threat to the stability of society.
The death penalty is a primitive ritual and should be abolished.

11.5 Letter writing ☆

One way in which people express their social attitudes is by writing to newspapers. Look at these examples and write a similar letter on a subject about which you feel strongly.

I hope, I am not the only one of your readers to be appalled by Gillian Widdicombe's description of how she was mugged in Chelsea (last week).

It seems obvious that prison sentences do not deter the violent criminal.

Capital punishment may not deter murder, but the motives for murder are complex and often clouded by extreme emotion.

By contrast, mugging is a mean and calculated crime.

I suggest that the potential mugger, who is probably a coward, would be deterred by the prospect of a whipping, followed by a short period, not in prison, but in a special hospital.

It does not require much imagination to think of more drastic and completely effective ways of deterring any second offenders.

The punishment of violence by greater violence may seem brutal, but surely it is justified if this is the only way to protect the physically weaker members of society from the brutality of thugs.

Tavistock. **J. H. S. Lang**

Sir,—We spend around £1,000 million a year on the results of family breakdown (Society Tomorrow, December 17). The Government grant to the National Marriage Guidance Council is nowhere near £1 million.

Even a doubling of this would enable far more to be done: in wider research into those social and personal changes which help or hinder family life; an education programme with schools and other organisations to overcome the lamentable lack of preparation noted by A. J. Brayshaw; a substantial increase in the number of counsellors

It is the children of broken or inadequate homes who go on to find the most difficulty in making happy and lasting relationships. Do we want to see these patterns of breakdown reproduced until our supremacy in the divorce stakes is assured?

Donald Godden.
National Marriage
Guidance Council,
Bristol.

Sir, — One would have thought that the cause of Miss Lindi St. Claire, the London prostitute, is one our Women's Libbers would embrace. She herself makes it clear that she is not an exploited female, the object of men's lusts, but an enterprising provider of humane services to the weaker members of the male sex. Yet what is virtually a social service, and certainly the oldest known to civilisation, is treated with that specific hypocrisy for which the English are infamous.

How different from the West German code of conduct. Hamburg's red light district, is regarded by the local authorities as a genuine place of business. The kindly ladies who spend their working hours there pay income tax, and receive the allowances which are their due. At the end of the day, they leave their "offices" and return to apartments in respectable buildings in the residential areas of the city.

Since prostitution is a trade which it is impossible to abolish, is it not more civilised to control it, than to close one's eyes to reality, and to pretend that it does not exist? This view may be regarded as a "foreigner's" shocking opinion, but as we are part of the European Community, it is hard to understand why we should spurn the "mores" which the other members find acceptable. — Yours faithfully,
J. L. Hendeles.
10 Cedars Close,
London NW4

11.6 Role-play: always welcome

Look at the cartoon opposite. It is sometimes difficult to live up to our ideals and put our principles into practice. Are you guilty? Do you know anyone who is? Think of a situation in which you might have trouble hiding your real feelings and improvise the scene.
Some suggestions:
A staunch socialist sends his or her children to a private school.
A pacifist spanks his or her children.
A heavy drinker fights against the legalisation of soft drugs.
A progressive factory owner has trouble in his or her factory.

> *Useful language*
>
> Justifying oneself:
>   It's not just that I think that state schools are worse than private ones.
>   It's just that there isn't one near us.
>   It's just because the private school is a lot more convenient.
>   It would be a pity not to give my child the best opportunities in life.
>   It would be a pity if he / she dropped out of school just because of my beliefs.

11.7 Discussion

Do we inherit attitudes from our parents?
Do we always fight against our parents when we are young?
Do people get more broad-minded as they get older?
Is the trend to the right as we get older inevitable?
Do you mix with people of the same type as yourself or with people who have different attitudes from your own?
Do you always try to convince other people of your own ideas?
How tolerant are you of other people's attitudes?

12 Laughing matters

12.1 Your sense of humour ☆

Do you think you have got an above-average sense of humour? If so, you are one of the 98% of the population who believe they have!
If you want to know more about your type of humour, look at the following cartoon drawings and grade them on the following scale. Work with a partner, but score individually.

5 = hilarious
4 = very funny
3 = quite funny
2 = slightly funny
1 = not funny at all

a)

Drawing by Chas. Addams;
© 1940, 1968 The New Yorker Magazine, Inc.

b)

c)

"I can't stand him, really, but I quite like dressing him up."

d)

"Poor Brendon—he never stood a chance."

e)

"Magic? Who said anything about magic?"

f)

g)

"I'd say loosen his flies but who listens to sex therapists?"

h)

"My man don't wrestle till we hear it talk."

Drawing by Richard Decker; © 1934, 1962 The New Yorker Magazine, Inc.

i)

j)

"Do you mind turning down the volume?"

k)

Drawing by O. Soglow;
© 1965, The New Yorker Magazine, Inc.

l)

"Look, if it upsets you so much, Harry . . ."

m)

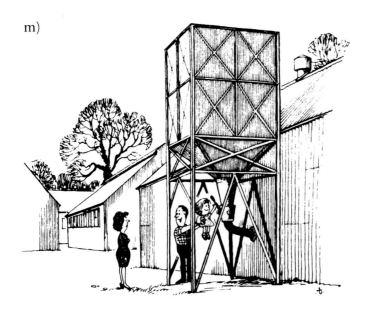

"She loves feeding the animals."

n)

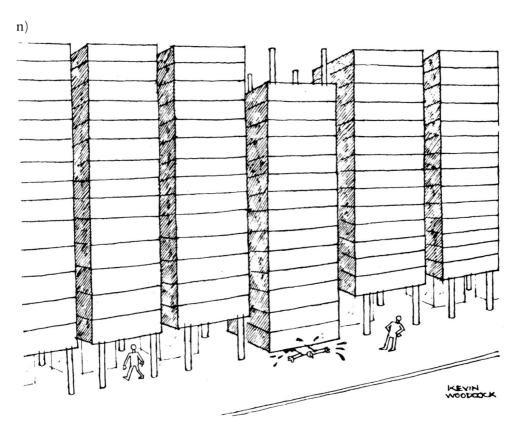

o)

'The prisoner wonders if you would mind wearing these for the first fifty?'

The basic 'joke' in each of these drawings fits into one of five categories of humour, though in some cases a secondary source of humour is present and the cartoon overlaps two or more categories. These five categories are: *nonsense humour* in which the effect relies mainly on incongruous or improbable elements; more or less explicit *sexual jokes*; *satire* in which people or institutions are held up to ridicule; *aggressive jokes*, which include physical violence, brutality, torture or sadism; and finally, that more sophisticated version of aggressive humour, *black humour*, which mingles the unpleasant, the absurd and often even taboo subjects to produce rather more grim laughter.

Nonsense humour: a, f, k.
Sexual jokes: it is not possible to provide here sufficiently explicit sexual jokes for this category to give a very accurate picture of this kind of humour. The jokes which rely at least partly on sex are b, g, l.
Satirical jokes: c, h, m.
Aggressive jokes: e, j, o.
Black humour: d, i, n.

By adding your score together in each of these categories (minimum 3, maximum 15) you will rapidly see which kind of joke you find most funny. If you scored highly on satire, you may have been sensitive to the satire in the sexual jokes. If you scored highly in the aggressive category, you probably also scored above average in the black humour drawings. Black humour can also be related to nonsense humour, as is the case in d and n, and can occur in sexual jokes such as b. If you scored more than 40 over all of these five broad categories you probably have an average sense of humour. If you scored very highly indeed, this might mean that you have a 'good sense of humour', but it might also mean that you are rather indiscriminate.

Bring other cartoons to class and classify them. Do they fit into the categories above, or do you need other categories?

12.2 What's in a joke ☆

There are many different types of jokes. Here are a few examples:

a) The 'nonsense' pun, very popular with schoolchildren. Can you work these out?

Waiter, waiter, what soup is this?
It's bean soup, sir.
I don't care what it was. I want to know what it is now.

Waiter, waiter, what's wrong with these eggs?
I don't know, sir. I only laid the table.

Waiter, waiter, will the pancakes be long?
No, sir, round.

Waiter, waiter, what's this fly doing in my soup?
The breaststroke, I think, sir.

Doctor, doctor, will you help me out?
Certainly, which way did you come in?

Teacher: I wish you'd pay a little attention.
Pupil: I'm paying as little as I can.

Did you hear about the teacher who was cross-eyed?
She couldn't control her pupils.

Teacher: You should have been here at 9 o'clock.
Small boy: Why, what happened?

b) Riddles based on the same kind of nonsense pun:

What do you call an Arabian dairy farmer?
A milk sheik.

What sort of robbery is the easiest?
A safe robbery.

What's the best system of book-keeping?
Never lend them.

Which is the fastest, heat or cold?
Heat, because you can catch cold.

A barrel of beer fell on a man. Why wasn't he hurt?
It was light ale.

What did the barman say when the ghost asked for a drink?
Sorry, we don't serve spirits.

Why are policemen strong?
Because they can hold up traffic.

Which driver never commits a traffic offence?
A screwdriver.

What do you call a bull asleep on the ground?
A bulldozer.

How many did you get?

12.3 The best joke

The jokes above depend on a certain use of language. There are lots of other sorts of jokes. Most countries have ethnic jokes about their neighbours. There are nonsense stories, satirical jokes, sexual jokes, shaggy dog stories and so on. Organise a joke competition in your class. Each person tells a joke and the class votes for the funniest.

12.4 Caricatures ☆

The exaggerated portrait of an individual or a class of individuals is a rich source of humour. Two examples that spring to mind are the English City gentleman with his bowler hat and pin-striped suit, or the absent-minded professor with his glasses and balding head.
a) In groups of two or three, prepare a sketch, a mime or a monologue based on a person, or a type of person, that is well-known in your country. Act out what you have prepared to another group, which should guess who you are caricaturing. Discuss which elements of the person were useful in making your performance a success and which elements were not fully exploited.

b) Can you write a short, comical description of yourself? Try! Make the description anonymous. Members of the class can then read the descriptions out to see if the writers can be recognised.

12.5 ☆

WELL, JUST HOW AMBITIOUS AND THRUSTING ARE YOU?

A special Punch survey

1. Recently a New Society survey suggested that most Britons lack ambition and are happy just to drift along, doing enough to make ends meet. Which of the following most nearly describes your reaction?

- ☐ Yes
- ☐ Mmm
- ☐ Well, yes but
- ☐ Oh, I don't know, though
- ☐ It's people like that who are ruining a once great country
- ☐ It's magazines like that which are ruining a once readable country
- ☐ If you people at Punch really think I'm going to sit down and put ticks in these silly little boxes, you can think again.

2. When people stop you in the street armed with clip-boards and cheap ball-point pens, do you

- ☐ Answer their dreary questions about your smoking/shaving/travelling habits because it makes you feel the centre of attention?
- ☐ Answer their dreary questions about your smoking/shaving/travelling habits because you enjoy giving totally misleading answers?
- ☐ Answer the questions and nick the ball-point pen?
- ☐ Push them under a passing bus?
- ☐ Suddenly lose your faculty for speaking English and become a Persian tourist?

3. Do you ever get the feeling these days that

- ☐ Half the world seems to spend its time organising questionnaires?
- ☐ The other half spends its time answering them?
- ☐ Statistics are the brandy of the bureaucrat?
- ☐ 98.4% of all questions leave only a space for a Yes or No answer when the real reply should be, Only on Saturdays or, Not if I've just had a Flaming Row with the Wife?
- ☐ Only people without ambition or drive ever answer surveys?
- ☐ The other half become sociologists and therefore unemployable?

4. Do you consider quartz digital watches to be

- ☐ An advance, because they do all the work?
- ☐ A step backwards, because they need two hands to operate?
- ☐ Unlikely to replace sun-dials?
- ☐ Another Swiss gimmick, soon to be provided with musical tunes and/or cuckoos?
- ☐ The most boring subject of conversation since mortgages?
- ☐ The prelude to speaking thermometers?

5. Are the followers of punk rock

- ☐ Disadvantaged young members of society creating their own culture for themselves?
- ☐ Yobs?

⟫→

- ☐ Cheap copy for unoriginal journalists?
- ☐ Going to be middle-aged and parents of families in two months time?
- ☐ Hidden under stones during the day-time?
- ☐ Your children, whom you mistakenly thought to be down the youth club?

6. When you see a sign reading SKATE BOARDING PROHIBITED, do you think
   - ☐ Bloody authorities?
   - ☐ Bloody kids?
   - ☐ How on earth does one board a skate?

7. As an example of real guts, ambition and British enterprise, would you single out
   - ☐ Concorde?
   - ☐ Re-issuing old Beatles concerts?
   - ☐ The Channel Tunnel?
   - ☐ Asians keeping the local corner shop open till late at night?

8. When you are told that a great national debate has been set in motion on, say, education, do you
   - ☐ Get down the pub and have a great debate
   - ☐ Switch off BBC2?
   - ☐ Go out into the country and have a lovely day fishing, far from the office, who all think you are at a football match anyway
   - ☐ Go to granny's funeral and have a lovely time far from the office, who all think you are at a football match anyway
   - ☐ Feel surprised when the national debate unaccountably fails to make the newspapers?

9. When you are asked to fill in the answers to a grand national survey on British attitudes, your immediate reaction is to
   - ☐ Fill in **all** the boxes
   - ☐ Throw yourself under a bus
   - ☐ Take up Yoga
   - ☐ Count your fingers
   - ☐ Stare into space
   - ☐ Get down the pub and get pissed

nick: steal
yobs: uncouth youngsters
guts: courage
get pissed: (slang) get drunk

Results

If you have filled in one box in each section, you are dull, predictable and lacking in ambition.
If you have left all the boxes unfilled, you are predictable, dull and lacking in ambition. If you switched to another article as soon as you saw that this was yet another survey, then there is hope for you yet. Not much, though.

How far did you get before you realised this was a joke? This questionnaire comes from *Punch*, a magazine which has been a weekly source of amusement to the British for many years. Do you think it's funny or just plain silly?

12.6 Discussion

What do we laugh at and why?
Can one define humour? Do you know of writers and philosophers who have tried to do so?
Are there national variations in humour?
Are people who make us laugh a lot really pessimists or optimists?
What are your favourite comic books? What films and what cartoons make you laugh the most?

Answers and scoring instructions

1.1 Do you see yourself as others see you?

Points:
1 (a) 2 (b) 4 (c) 6
2 (a) 6 (b) 4 (c) 7 (d) 2 (e) 1
3 (a) 4 (b) 2 (c) 5 (d) 7 (e) 6 (f) 1
4 (a) 4 (b) 6 (c) 2 (d) 1
5 (a) 6 (b) 4 (c) 3 (d) 5 (e) 2
6 (a) 6 (b) 4 (c) 2
7 (a) 6 (b) 2 (c) 4
8 (a) 6 (b) 2 (c) 7 (d) 3 (e) 5 (f) 1 (g) 4
9 (a) 7 (b) 6 (c) 4 (d) 2 (e) 1
10 (a) 4 (b) 2 (c) 3 (d) 7 (e) 5 (f) 6 (g) 1

3.7 Surprise quiz

Scoring: One point for each answer that agrees with those given below.
1 True
2 False
3 False
4 False
5 True
6 True
7 False
8 False
9 False
10 True
11 True
12 False (no such word exists)
13 True
14 True
15 True

Average score: 10

4.1 Fighting fit

1 False. This is a common misunderstanding, but in fact moderate physical exercise does not stimulate the appetite. Research even suggests that an increase in physical activity in normally sedentary people may actually make them want to eat less.
2 False. Fat does not change into muscle any more than muscle changes into fat. Fat comes from the calories you consume in excess of those you need. If muscles are not used they may shrink. When you exercise, muscle tissue develops while fat tissue diminishes.
3 False. You lose no fat tissue through sweating, only fluid which is replaced very quickly by normal thirst.
4 False. Vitamins do not contain energy. They help to metabolise food into energy. Most people get all the vitamins they need if they eat a well-balanced diet. There is, for example, sufficient vitamin C in two pounds of oranges for the average person for a whole week. There is therefore no point in taking extra vitamins, and an excess of vitamins A and D can be harmful.
5 True – but with diet alone you lose muscle tissue as well as fat. When you exercise as well, most of the weight lost is fat.
6 True. This size bar of chocolate contains about 550 calories and walking at this pace you burn about 250 calories an hour. You could alternatively cycle at 13 m.p.h. for 50 minutes to obtain the same result!
7 False. It is calories, not carbohydrates, that make people fat. Some carbohydrates, such as bread and potatoes, actually contain fewer calories per ounce than sirloin steaks or roast beef.

8   False. Dairy foods, eggs, and some vegetables are perfectly acceptable alternatives to meat or fish.
9   False. You would be cutting out very good sources of several B vitamins, vitamin C, and other nutrients by eliminating such starchy foods as peas, potatoes, bread, and cereals from your diet.
10 False. It is what you eat, not when you eat, that makes you fat. Light meals and snacks of fruit, nuts or cereals are probably better for you than three large meals a day. Biscuits, cakes and chocolate are disastrous whether eaten between meals or at mealtimes.
11 True. Your body has a biological rhythm and does not metabolise food in the same way at every point in the cycle of roughly 24 hours. Food eaten before 3 p.m. will be consumed by the organism, whereas food eaten in the evening will stock up the body's reserves, i.e. become fat.
12 False. Just variety is not enough. To provide the body with the calories, proteins, vitamins and minerals that it needs to keep you fit, you should have the following number of helpings from the four major food groups each day:
    Two or more servings from the *milk* group (milk, cheese, yoghurt and other dairy foods).
    Two or more from the *meat* group (meat, poultry, fish, eggs and meat alternatives such as dried beans, lentils and nuts).
    Four or more from the *bread* group (bread, cereal, noodles and other grain products).
    Four or more from the *vegetable* group (vegetables and fruit).
13 False. Alcohol helps you fall asleep, but it also stops you dreaming in the first part of the night. As the amount you dream overall is the same, the second part of the night will be more agitated, with nightmares and so on. A glass of warm milk or a few deep breathing exercises would be much better for you!
14 False. The average need is seven hours a night. If you sleep more than nine hours a night your life expectancy will be considerably shortened.
15 True. Most people sleep too much rather than too little, but people who sleep less than five hours run the same risk as those who sleep more than nine hours.
16 True. Laughter dilates the neuro-vegetal centres and releases adrenalin which stimulates the pulse, the circulation of the blood, etc.

6.1 Good taste

Scoring: Give yourself 3 points for each correct answer in Part 1; 2 points for each correct answer in Part 2.

Part 1		Part 2	
1	second	1	b
2	third	2	b
3	third	3	a
4	first	4	b
5	third	5	b
6	third	6	b
7	third	7	b
8	first	8	b
9	first	9	b
10	second	10	a

7.1 What's your brain power?

1. Answer: 30 squares.
   Once you saw beyond the obvious answer – 16 – or perhaps 17 (if you counted the square that contains the smaller ones) – you were on your way to solving the problem.

2. Psychologist Norman R. Maier indicates that most solutions to this problem fall into four broad categories, and each category requires a switch in perceptual viewpoint:
   Category A: If you see the problem in terms of 'inadequate reach,' then the solutions involve extending your reach by means of a cane, umbrella, stick, pole or some other object with a handle.
   Category B: If you perceive the problem as 'the strings are too short,' then your solutions call for ways to extend the length of the strings, for example, tying another string, a belt, windowshade cord, ruler or other object to them.
   Category C: If you feel that 'one string won't stay in the middle while I reach for the other,' your solutions involve ways to tie one string down in the center, either to a high-back chair or a stepladder, or any other object that you can readily move around.
   Category D: If you perceive the problem as 'the second string won't come to me while I'm holding the first,' then your solutions could involve utilising a fan, opening windows or doors to create a breeze, tying magnets to the strings, or tying a ring, key or some other object to the string, and swinging it like a pendulum.
   If your solutions entailed all four categories, you're displaying extraordinary versatility and flexibility in your thinking.

3. (a) The difference between the ages is 32 years, so I am 32 since my mother is twice as old.
   (b) 99 9/9
   (c) ```
        888
         88
          8
          8
          8
       ————
       1000
       ```

4. (a) One hour. The alarm would go off at 9 that night.
   (b) All 11 months.
   (c) He is still living.
   (d) Hold the egg up and drop it from a height of 6 feet. It will drop 5 feet without breaking. After that you will need to clean up the mess.
   (e) The 2 fathers and 2 sons were: A son, his father and his father's father.
   (f) Only once. After the first time, you're subtracting from 22, then 20, and so on.
   (g) One sizeable haystack.
   (h) If you're governed by the profit motive, you'd choose half a truckload of dimes, since they're smaller and worth twice as much.
   (i) They could all take turns and sit on your lap. You certainly couldn't accomplish that.
   (j) Her hat was hung over the end of the gun.
       ```

7.2 Pure logic

1. Among the 97 per cent of the women, if half wear two earrings and half none, this is the same as if each wore one. Assuming that each of the 800 women is wearing one earring, there are 800 earrings.
2. Each barber must have cut the other's hair. The logician picked the barber who had given his rival the better haircut.
3. Nil. If three letters match the envelopes, so will the fourth.
4. Three apples.
5. £13,212.
6. Eighty minutes is the same as one hour and 20 minutes.
7. The customer had sugared his coffee before he found the fly.
8. The parrot was deaf.

7.3 A famour puzzler's logic

A. Babies cannot manage crocodiles.
B. *Your* presents to me are not made of tin.
C. All my potatoes in this dish are old ones.
D. None of *your* sons are fit to serve on a jury.
E. Jenkins is inexperienced.
F. No hedge-hog takes in *The Times*.
G. This dish is unwholesome.
H. No jugs in this cupboard will hold water.

7.9 Are you a genius?

1. c. Omit the horizontal line in the asterisk, as it was omitted in the circle.
2. c.
3. e. The other words are nouns.
4. d and e.
5. 49; 9 is 3 squared, 16 is 4 squared, 25 is 5 squared, and so on. Also, 9 + 7 = 16 + 9 = 25, 25 + 11 = 36, and so on.
6. Earth.
7. 2. In each vertical and horizontal row, the second number is subtracted from the first.
8. Present.
9. b and c. All the others hold things together.
10. c. A whirlpool is part of the sea as a mountain is part of land.
11. 33. The difference between the numbers is progressively multiplied by 2.
12. b and d.
13. e.
14. 240. (24 × 10 and 12 × 20 both equal 240).
15. 768. It is not necessary to determine the values of A, B, C, D. Simply multiply 24 × 32.
16. d. The ball gets larger in each box, while the triangle remains the same size, and the ball and the triangle keep alternating positions.
17. e. The others are all things that increase images or sounds.
18. a and d are synonyms.
19. a. Just the fact that Jim can't see a service station ahead doesn't mean there isn't one.
20. c. Positive and minus change positions; neutral stays in the same place.

8.1 Your superstitious beliefs – a quick check

Points:
For every no: 0
For every yes: 2
For every doubtful answer: 1

9.3 Thumbnail portraits

Example 1 goes with personality D; 2 with A; 3 with C; 4 with B. The commonest errors are mismatches of 3 with A and 2 with C.

9.4 Feminine writing and masculine writing

a) is male and b) and c) are female. The top and bottom examples are usually identified fairly easily, but the middle example is more of a puzzle. The clue upon which judgement is based seems to be circularity.

10.3 Your childhood

Question	a	b	c	d
1	6	3	4	1
2	5	3	1	
3	3	5	1	
4	3	2	5	1
5	2	3	5	
6	3	4	5	
7	1	4	3	5
8	3	1	2	5
9	4	3	1	
10	5	3	1	

10.5 Are you a good judge of character?

Score one point for every correct answer.
1b   7c
2c   8b
3a   9c
4b   10c
5c   11c
6b   12c

11.1 What's your opinion?

For questions 1, 2, 3, 6, 8, 11, 12, 13, 18, 19: $++ = 5, + = 4, 0 = 3, - = 2, -- = 1$.
For questions 4, 5, 7, 9, 10, 14, 15, 16, 17, 20: $++ = 1, + = 2, 0 = 3, - = 4, -- = 5$.

Guidelines for teachers and students working alone

The material in this book is intentionally flexible in design. The level of learners, whether they are working alone or as part of a group, will determine the best use to which each unit may be put. In the latter case, the nature of the group, whether of uniform or mixed ability, will also be a factor.

One example of the way in which the material can be adapted is the main quiz in each unit. It will be a reading exercise for self-study students to which they must respond actively. It will serve the same purpose for a lower level group, but will involve discussion of meaning and fact at the same time. For higher level groups it should act as a springboard for discussion on a broader plane. In view of this diversity of aim, the instructions for the various activities throughout the units have been left as simple as possible. To interpret them for their own situation, the teacher and the student working alone should find the following guidelines helpful.

To the student

As you work through the units in this book, you will be learning or revising the language of many aspects of everyday life. The quizzes are designed so that you do not just read them passively, but react to them and find out how they apply to you. If you can try some of them out on a friend, a colleague or a member of the family, all the better. It will serve as reinforcement to your own learning. Most people can, in fact, find someone who is happy to learn a little English provided that the task is not too arduous and is even enjoyable – and one of the aims of this book is to make learning a pleasant process.

If you can find someone to work with you regularly, you will find the work more stimulating and be able to do some of the pair and group work. If you are able to do this, do not worry about not having a teacher to correct your mistakes. You will be developing fluency and will gradually become aware of areas of learning that are a problem to you and things you are not sure of. You should list these as you work, and consult a grammar book, a dictionary or a native speaker of English when you have the opportunity to do so. If you wish to do some more systematic grammar work, you will find the chart on page 113 helpful. It will indicate which section of a grammar book you should consult. It is worth attempting the writing tasks even if you can find no-one to correct them, for they will help you check how much you remember. You can even try talking to yourself – particularly if you have a cassette recorder so that you can record yourself!

Lastly, this is not a grammar book and it is not meant to be memorised from A to Z. Rather, it is meant to capture your genuine interest and give you a certain amount of fun and enjoyment, as well as enabling you to improve your English. It should also give you ideas as to the kind of authentic language material that you can learn from, and make a change from the long and difficult newspaper articles that many learners rely on for keeping up their English.

To the teacher

These guidelines are divided into four parts: 1) general points concerning the methodological approach to teaching and learning that underlie the material; 2) notes on the types of exercise to be found in each unit: reading tasks, pair work, role-play, group work, writing tasks and discussion; 3) notes on specific points in each unit; 4) notes on the useful language sections and the chart which enables the book to be linked up with a main course book from a thematic, functional or structural point of view.

General guidelines

The material in this book is to a great extent designed to be used by students working in pairs or in small groups. Consequently, the role of the teacher is not so much to give a model of fluency in the target language as to encourage fluency in the learner. It is less to explain words and grammatical structures than to act as a facilitator, enabling the learners to work these things out for themselves. The teacher will present the material, organise the classroom, keep the students working and smooth out the difficulties they meet. Above all, he or she will observe the learning process and will discover where the real difficulties lie for individual learners.

The kind of classroom in which there is an empty space or in which the furniture can be moved is particularly suitable for the material in this book. The learners will be able to move around to form new pairs and new work groups. As they do this they should be encouraged to stretch and yawn in order to renew their mental energy levels! In a traditional classroom, students will work with their immediate neighbours, on both sides as well as in front and behind.

Some students will want to spend much longer on the activities in the book than others. This is particularly true of mixed ability classes. When this happens, the faster students should be asked to do other activities in the unit or the writing exercises, or they should be encouraged to invent activities of their own. It is a good idea to set a time limit in any case, as some students will never finish a task otherwise.

The teacher who feels that this kind of material may entail a high level of chaos and noise should be reassured. Students who are at least partly responsible for what they are doing tend to be more involved in their learning and noise levels remain under control. If the instructions are clear at the outset, the students soon acquire good independent learning habits and may even at some stage take over the organisation of the class if the teacher wishes. Through working in this manner, the students will acquire autonomous learning skills which will stand them in good stead for the future when they may have to keep up their English without the help of a teacher.

Finally, a word about the content of the book. The learners are asked to talk about themselves, and the subjects dealt with are often highly personal. If this is, on the one hand, likely to motivate them, it may, on the other hand, be an occasional source of worry and inhibition. Consequently the learners should be reminded that they are not at Scotland Yard but in a language classroom, and that there is no obligation to tell the truth if they do not wish to reveal their true personalities! Teachers who do not know their classes very well are advised to give certain activities for homework, or to avoid them altogether.

Types of exercise

READING TEXTS (QUIZZES AND QUESTIONNAIRES)

In an advanced intermediate class in which the learners are used to talking in the target language, the quiz will serve as a springboard for general discussion on the topic. The students will work through it, in pairs or small groups, without any preparation. Some intermediate classes, even at an advanced stage, have trouble sticking to the target language on topics which are personal, because they become carried away by the subject matter. In this case the teacher should insist on pairs rather than groups. Another simple remedy to this problem is to ensure that only one student in each pair has the book open at this stage. He or she will then quiz his / her partner by reading out the questions or reformulating them in his / her own words. This tactic should also be adopted in cases where students are not used to working together and tend to isolate themselves with their questionnaire rather than discuss the issues with their partner.

In lower intermediate classes the questionnaire will essentially be a reading task and a longer and quieter activity. Learners may work with a dictionary or a vocabulary sheet, and discuss both the language and the facts in their own language, asking the teacher for explanations when necessary. This type of group would occasionally benefit from a more lively presentation stage to focus their interest. The following suggestions may be adopted:

a) The teacher brings into the classroom photos or pictures related to the topic. The learners, either as a class or in small groups, discuss preferences, likes and dislikes, etc. Pictures of people, food or sport would be suitable for unit 4 for example, and well-dressed people or attractive interiors (or the opposite!) for unit 6 and different types of advertising for unit 3.

b) The teacher can 'feed in' some of the information to one or two students before the class or during the break. These students will then pass on the information to small groups afterwards. The 'pure logic' stories in unit 7, the anecdotes in unit 8 or the jokes in unit 12 are suitable for this type of presentation.

c) Use a 'milling exercise' to get the class sorted into random pairs or groups. The questions and answers to the riddles in unit 12 can be copied onto separate cards and one given to each student. The students then go round the class checking each other's cards till they find the one that matches. Other suggestions for forming pairs or groups are: matching famous personalities (unit 11): the name of a sport with a piece of equipment associated with it (unit 4); different elements of a well-balanced meal (unit 4); members of a family (unit 10); items of a well-designed outfit (unit 6).

d) Any of the activities described in the pair work section of these notes, below.

In some lower intermediate classes the learners are as much in need of listening comprehension practice as reading exercises. Several of the units in this book can be presented as listening comprehension; for example, the descriptions of the lines on the hand in unit 2, the brain power exercises in unit 7, and the questions and analyses in some other units such as the family quiz in unit 10.

Such a listening comprehension exercise can be done in one of the following ways: a) the teacher reads out the text directly to the students; b) if a cassette recorder is available, the teacher can pre-record the text and play it to the class. If several cassette players are available the students can listen in small groups; c) if a language laboratory is available, the exercise can be done individually and impressions compared afterwards.

The information in the quizzes has been gathered from reliable sources. However, the students may disagree, dispute facts, and generally know a lot about certain subjects. They should be encouraged to criticise, comment and share any extra information they may have with the rest of the class. Such an occasion is an all too rare opportunity for authentic discussion in the classroom and should be welcomed by the teacher.

Suggestions for coping with the difficult vocabulary in the reading texts are to be found in the useful language section of these notes, on page 111.

PAIR WORK

As far as possible the teacher should allow the students to form pairs naturally. He or she may need to resort to artificial means or be dictatorial if the situation arises where the same students always work together, or when some 'recurring' pairs are obviously ill-suited for working together.

If the learners continually resort to their native language during this stage despite repeated exhortation on the part of the teacher not to do so, some more straightforward factual pair work may be needed to start with. The following suggestions may be useful:

a) *Anecdotes* Each student in the pair relates in turn an anecdote connected with the topic (a dishonest anecdote, unit 3; a supernatural story or a dream, unit 8; the best or worst day of their childhood, unit 10; the funniest thing that ever happened, unit 12). Students can either improvise or be asked to prepare such an anecdote for homework.

b) *Drawing games* One student gets the other to draw according to his or her instructions. For example, the lines on one's hand, unit 2; a picture or the plan of a house, unit 6; a cartoon, unit 12.

c) *Guessing games* i) One student chooses a person related to the topic (a famous sportsman or chef in unit 4; a designer of clothes or interiors in unit 6; a politician or social figure in unit 11, etc.). The other student asks questions about the person's identity, which may only be answered by yes or no, until he or she guesses who it is. ii) One student describes such a famous person until the other student guesses who it is. The second student may be given instructions to be a little simple and not guess too quickly in order to encourage his or her partner to talk.

d) *Information transfer exercises* One student has information on a card, the other a plan or a chart on which he or she must write the information the first student communicates to him or her. One example is the UFO report sheet in unit 8, but other simple exercises can be invented. For example, through a description of the food in the canteen during the previous week the second student must work out the exact menus for each day. One student may have the arrangement of the furniture in a house on a card and the other student must draw it in on an empty plan. Budget figures and statistics of various kinds also lend themselves to this kind of activity.

e) *What's the difference game* Two students are each given a picture which is identical except that three or four details have been changed. The students must find out what these differences are by describing their picture. Once again, the picture can be chosen according to the theme of the unit (two different palm line drawings in unit 2; a house or a person with several details changed in unit 6; a family in unit 10; a cartoon in unit 12).

ROLE-PLAY

Though many people enjoy the acting element in role-play, many others do not. The objections most often raised are the dislike of giving a performance and the difficulty of projecting oneself into another personality. Consequently, the role-plays in this book are all designed to be carried out simultaneously in pairs or small groups, with characters that will fit the student's own personality. Thinking about and discussing the way the character will play the role, especially if this involves thinking about how the student would react in such a situation, is an integral part of the activity and is a good opening to the study of register. The students should be allowed to choose their own roles.

WRITING TASKS

Even if the students are only interested in learning to speak English, writing is a useful way of consolidating one's knowledge. These tasks are probably best done for homework.

DISCUSSION

Discussion in small groups is the best solution unless the noise level is bothering your colleagues or your students resolutely refuse to speak English. Shy students are less inhibited in small groups, also the speaking time allotted to each student is obviously greater. If you want to conclude the discussion with the whole class together, it is a good idea to pool group conclusions in the last few minutes. Encourage the students to be as concrete as possible in their discussion. They will reach abstract ideas through anecdote rather than the other way round.

GROUP WORK

Unless otherwise specified, this is intended for groups of between three and five students. Students usually work better in groups which they compose themselves through natural affinity. However, in a situation in which the same people insist on working together, or in which particular groups do not seem to be working efficiently, it may be necessary for the teacher to set up the groups. It is often a good idea to do this in a random fashion. Students can number off (1–3 for groups of three, 1–4 for groups of four, etc.). Then all the ones, all the twos, all the threes etc. join up to work together. Playing cards can also be distributed. All the hearts or clubs, or all the jacks and queens join up in a group. Discussing how successfully – or unsuccessfully – each group has accomplished its task is a valuable source of feedback and a rare moment of authentic communication in the classroom. It should be done as often as possible.

Notes on individual units

Unit 1   If you have a class in which the learners do not know each other at all, you should leave the quiz 1.3, Mutual impressions, until later on in the course.

Unit 2   If you have access to a photocopier, you can introduce this unit by providing a photocopy of your own hand or by making a set of photocopies of the whole class's hands. Interpretations of unknown hands can thus be made, introducing more fun into the exercise when the impressions are compared with reality.

Unit 3   If your class is relaxed and the members know each other well, you can introduce this unit by getting the students, in small groups, to recount a dishonest anecdote in which they were involved. Alternatively, the anecdote may remain anonymous.

Unit 4   Activity 4.3, Overweight? Underweight?, can be extended to include comparisons of shoe, shirt and dress sizes, etc. If you feel at ease with your class, you can take in a couple of tape measures and get the members to compare waist sizes and so on.

Unit 5   If the members of your class wish, they can make the role-play, 5.3, Taking it easy, more personal, and act out themselves giving advice to a friend.

Unit 6   For activity 6.5, The rules of good taste, you will find a pile of fashion or interior design magazines useful for the students to browse through as they work. These may have to be local magazines if British or American ones are not available.

Unit 7   The brain power exercises and the pure logic stories may not generate very much discussion. They are better used as pair work when one student has the book open and asks the question, only hinting at the answer if his or her partner is really stuck. The diagrams in 7.1 can be copied onto the blackboard or one learner can describe them to the other who then draws them. The logic stories can also be used as straightforward listening comprehension.

Unit 8 One main area of dreaming is sex. This aspect has been removed from the quiz in 8.7, The 'night' side of life, in order not to embarrass certain cultures. If your students talk freely, encourage them to talk about this subject, perhaps by suggesting that they think up categories of dreams that are not mentioned in the quiz.

Unit 9 Homework from a previous exercise can be distributed for graphological study in this unit. If you wish to keep the samples anonymous you should bear this in mind when setting the homework and ask the students not to write their names on their work.

Unit 10 If your class is very obviously single, you may like to leave 10.8, Somebody special, as optional homework.

Unit 11 Four students will need to prepare their participation in the debate in 11.4 for homework.

Unit 12 A set of cartoons from local sources could be used as an introduction, so that the learners define their own humour before considering the Anglo-Saxon variety.

Useful language sections

VOCABULARY

Useful expressions and vocabulary are offered as a resource to the student at certain points in the book. It is up to the individual teacher to decide whether to pre-teach these expressions or whether to encourage the students to find out meanings by providing, according to his or her means, a classroom set of dictionaries, a vocabulary sheet or translations on the blackboard that the students can consult as and when they need to. Students can also be encouraged to use the teacher as a walking dictionary when they come across words they do not know. Where no vocabulary list is offered it is usually because the relevant vocabulary is in the main quiz, where the same teaching alternatives apply. The teacher can identify what he or she considers to be problem words and pre-teach them or let the students use their own initiative. In either case, the students should be encouraged to distinguish between words that are likely to be useful to them in the future and for which an effort of memory is worthwhile, and those that they understand but will probably never need to use.

SPECIFIC FUNCTIONS

In each unit one or more specific functions are offered for study. In every case, the teacher may adopt one of the following courses of action:

a) Present the relevant structures to the students before carrying out the activity.

b) Hold a group inquiry after the activity is over to find out what language was missing. The suggested structures may appear more meaningful at this point.

c) Let the students consult the book without drawing overt attention to the structures offered. The students learn through practice alone.

There is of course no one-to-one relationship between functions and structures and the teacher may like to offer alternatives. Opportunities exist throughout the book for revising such basic functions as narrating, describing, commenting, asking questions, etc. The amount of explicit attention given to language work will depend on the teacher's own inclinations and the type of learner in the class.

THEME, FUNCTION AND STRUCTURE CHART

This chart offers suggestions as to how the material in this book may be integrated into a course. The starting point may be thematic, functional or structural. The structures that have been chosen for each language function are either basic ones that are still a source of problems to many intermediate students, or else structures that are usually presented at the upper intermediate stage.

Theme, function and structure chart

Unit	Theme	Function	Structure
1	Personal qualities, feelings, emotions, daily habits	Describing habits Giving advice	Simple present *should, ought to,* *to try doing* and *to try to do*
2	Personal qualities and characteristics	Predicting the future Talking about probability	Future tenses, and *likely to, bound to,* *it looks as if*
3	Honesty, social matters, money	Classifying activities Apologising, hedging	*–ing* forms as nouns, discourse markers, fillers
4	Food, exercise, the body, health, leisure, daily life, practice with figures	Making comparisons Polite disagreement	*the more ... the more*, etc. Negative question forms
5	Health, physical characteristics, behaviour, daily life events	Making suggestions Talking about the recent past	*should, ought to, might,* *had better* Present perfect, progressive aspect
6	Taste, colour, clothes, design, interior decorating, houses	Describing people Stating purposes Expressing doubt	Adjectives Infinitive with *to* Modals: *need, dare,* *be able to* (as a substitute for *can*)
7	Figures, elementary mathematical concepts, daily life	Making recommendations	Conditionals
8	Superstition, the subconscious, sleep and dreams	Talking about certainty and doubt Reporting an event	*must be / can't be, must have been, can't have been* Present perfect contrasted with simple past
9	Personal qualities and characteristics, jobs	Giving reasons and explanations Being emphatic	*on account of, because of, owing to* Adverbial adjuncts
10	Relations, friends, personality, domestic habits, social matters	Talking about people	*Someone interesting, someone to do something with* Modifiers other than *very* before a past participle
11	Social problems, politics	Formulating precise propositions Justifying oneself	Nouns in groups Constructions with *it*
12	Jokes, humour	Puns	Stress, concatenation